MW01599014

WONDERFUL ... you ENJOY ALL THINGS PSYSHIC & BEYOND Justis CHASE (handwritten inscription)

Cover Design Justis Chase

If you are unable to order this book from your local bookseller please go to www.thetenpermissions.com for ordering information or go to www.amazon.ca and order

ISBN-13:
978-1461106104

ISBN-10:
1461106109

To contact the author you can email Justis at:
justischase@gmail.com

Introduction.

Quantum science tells us that there are many dimensions in this world of vibration and illusion. Most of the time we are stuck in the one we find ourselves in now, but on some occasions things change and we can slip almost unknowing from one to another. And when we do we can discover great truths about our world, our beliefs and ourselves. This book will take you on such a journey. It will take you into a truth that exists just beyond the vibration of your sight and touch. If you ask, "is it real or fiction" you have missed the point entirely because it is neither. It's simply a post card from a fellow traveler telling you his story.

You will also notice that this book is short. It is not a long or complicated book Instead it is a book that will cause you to examine your own beliefs and your own journey.

If after reading this book you are unsure what it really is telling you then you are on the right path. It's not a text of rules to follow nor is it a guidebook to tell you how to live your life. It is here to take you on an adventure into another dimension, one as close as your breathing and as far away as your dreams.

This is not a book that I "decided" to write. It is a book that I lived and as such may not be grammatically correct in all aspects. If you believe that grammar must be perfect to understand a message then you may not be as pleased with this book as many others you have in your library.

This book is a look into another dimension. You can take from it what you want and leave the rest because it's not written to tell you something specific, but rather to introduce you to a place that is so close you can feel it and yet so difficult to find. So regardless of who you are if this book is in your hands then take the step and understand that it's in your hands for a reason.

In short this book is a story or parable, in any case its time for the story to start.

Chapter One

It was very late at night and I had been traveling for a long time, almost 15 hours and I knew I needed to stop. I was to the point that I was getting giddy and almost hallucinating at the same time. If I didn't pull off the road I would probably be in tomorrows newspaper obituary section. My mind drifted away from my driving as I imagined the short but emotive words. Traveler found dead in smoking wreck, apparently a victim of his own stupidity. He drove until he fell asleep at the wheel and crashed into a tree.

I was startled back into reality by the feel of the wheels on the side of the road. Sometime in the past road workers had cut slots into the side of the asphalt for cases just like mine. So when the tires hit them they rumbled and startled the occupant awake.

They did exactly what they were supposed to do and I found my eyes wide open as I pulled the car back onto the main part of the road.

It was at that moment that I spotted the light ahead on the side of the road. I knew that regardless of what it was I needed to pull over and get some sleep. If it meant that I had to sleep in the car so be it. I needed to pull over.

As I got closer I noticed that it was a small motel with a bar attached. I pulled into the parking lot and immediately noticed that the parking lot was full of motorcycles. Big dark motorcycles, Harley Davidson's mostly. I carefully negotiated the bikes lined up like fighter jets on an aircraft carrier and sleepily made my way to the motel door.

—

As I approached I noticed a torn piece of paper scotch-taped to the window of the door. As I got closer I could read in big printed letters running at an angle down the paper "IF YOU NEED A ROOM AFTER HOURS SEE THE BARTENDER"

I turned back from the door and started moving towards the music and light of the bar next door. Walking past the two dozen or so motorcycles I almost faltered and thought of getting back into my car and driving a mile or two further down the road and then pulling off but something seemed to be pulling me on in spite of my apprehension.

I opened the door and all eyes in the place swung around to meet mine. If there was ever a time when I felt totally out of place this was it. Everyone in the place was at least ten years my junior and every one I could see wore a motorcycle gang patch.

As the eyes followed me I knew that if I ran, which was what my tired brain was trying to get me to do, I would be set upon, so feigning courage, I stepped in and walked boldly up to bar and asked the bartender for a room.

The bar tender turned away as if to get something and I noticed the room noise started returning and I was beginning to feel almost comfortable when a powerful hand fell upon my shoulder. I turned to look and the owner of the hand stood at least ten inches taller than me and out weighed me by over a hundred pounds.
I turned back towards the bar to gauge the reaction of the bartender but was met with a shrug. Swinging my head back towards the stranger holding my shoulder I swallowed and hoped my terror was not as obvious outside of me as it was inside.

When my eyes met the huge man I noticed they sparkled and that he was not wearing the same clothes as the others. In fact, he was not dressed like a biker at all. Instead he was wearing a business suit of sorts and had a casual open neck shirt on. For a second I felt relief hoping that he wouldn't want to mess his clothes up with my blood but then the terror rose anew as I realized that a huge man with a beard, no matter how well dressed was unlikely to be friendly in a place like this.

My eyes met his for a moment and then I shut them tight, expecting the blow that I was sure would follow. Instead a deep voice echoed through to my fear enshrouded brain.

His voice was very mellow and almost melodic.

"Hey don't be so scared, there's nothing to be afraid of. I'm with you."

My eyes flew open and his hand was leading me towards a table in the back. As I followed along, being lead by his giant hand I noticed the table was not empty. It was covered with beer glasses and smoldering cigarettes sitting in an ashtray. Around the table sat six men, each as large as the one leading me.

As we approached they stood up. I could feel the terror again rising in my stomach and was sure that had it not been for the strong hand on my shoulder I would have fainted dead away at that moment. But instead of insults or threats they simply nodded their heads and moved away leaving the table empty.

The large hand dropped me onto the bench seat and then he took a seat across from me and looked directly into my eyes.

The music had resumed as had the conversations and it seemed that neither my large new friend nor I were even noticed any more.

He looked directly across at me and smiled. I expected that most of his teeth would be gone but instead he had a movie star smile.

"So I guess you were a bit scared?"

I nodded and swallowed again.

"Most people are when they don't know what's going on."

I nodded again.

He turned his body slightly sideways and I noticed how very strong he looked. I could see the outline of muscles I didn't even know people could have.

"So I guess you are wondering why I brought you here?" he casually commented.

I shook my head and mumbled "what?"

Obviously he wanted to talk to me but why he brought me to the table seemed a strange way to start.

He turned back to me answering my unasked question.

"No, not why I brought you to the table. Why I brought you here." He smiled broadly.

"You mean to the bar?" I stammered trying to imagine what the heck he was talking about.

He seemed to be having a lot of fun at my expense, but considering his size and the obvious power he held over the others it seemed a silly thing to challenge his authority. So I just tried to look as friendly as I could and waited for him to continue.

"No, actually I don't mean the bar. I mean here." He swung his arms around as if to indicate the whole place.

I was afraid immediately and my face screwed up in a look that I'm sure said you're nuts. I must be sitting with an asylum escapee I thought. That's why they're all scared of him. He's totally nuts and capable of anything.

"You really don't get it do you?" He asked as he moved forward laying his massive arms on the table in front of me.

I shook my head slowly. He was right. I really didn't get it at all.

"You're here for a purpose. You're here to learn something and then to write about it and get the message out. We brought you here, to this place."

I wasn't a writer and I was not, as far as I knew, anyone that anyone would listen to. But again, if this guy was an escapee and he scared the bikers enough for them to give up their table I was going to do my best to make sure I kept him talking. At least he wasn't killing me if he was talking.

"Don't be so scared." He laughed. "No body's going to kill you, at least not here tonight."

I felt a rush of relief and then a refocusing of the terror. Could it be that he was planning to kill me tomorrow or later in the week?

—

"I picked you because you don't already have a lot of belief baggage." He leaned closer as he said this. "And that will make it easier for you to understand what I'm about to show you."

I muscled up my courage and spoke. "What exactly is happening?"

"Great question and about time you started asking some questions, 'cause it's actually all about you." He replied.

I was totally puzzled by what he said. "So what is happening, what did you want to show me or tell me. I'm really tired and all I wanted to do was stop for the night and get some sleep."

"I know." He said. "The problem is that is just the story you were in, it's not what is actually happening, it's just what you thought was happening. You see the thing is," he paused for a moment, "often what we think is going on and what is really going on are two different things."

My fear had diminished somewhat and he was beginning to cast a spell of intrigue over me. Despite my tiredness and fear there was something almost perfect about him. I was drawn to him, his manner and his words somehow.

"There is a big biker party down the road. This is just the warm up here and I want you to come with me to experience something."

Oh my. My stomach flipped and the terror returned. I was almost sick with tiredness and fear and at the same time I knew that I really didn't have a choice.

"Oh but you do." he answered, again without my question even being spoken.

"You have free choice. You can get up and walk out that door, or you can walk to the bar and get your key," he nodded to the bartender who swung a key around on his finger when I looked in his direction, "or you can simply accept that you are now part of something bigger than yourself and come see what I want you to see."

He sat back and seemed to be waiting for my answer. I gazed around the bar and looked back at him. I was already so tired I could hardly see straight and I knew I needed sleep. I was also scared out of my wits but something about him seemed to draw me to go along with what he wanted me to do so without fully understanding why, I nodded my head. "Lets go." I said.

Chapter Two

A few minutes later I was sitting on the back of his motorcycle riding down the highway into the night. We turned off the main road and onto a secondary dirt road. In the distance I could hear the sounds of motorcycles being gunned and loud laughter. Then I heard some screams over the rumble of the bikes. My blood turned to ice as I realized I had left the slight safety of the bar for a darkened road and bloodthirsty bikers. No one would know where I went. They would find my car a few days from now and ask around. I doubted that anyone in the bar would tell the police anything about my leaving. I would become one of the thousands of missing persons that simply disappear from their worlds never to be seen again.

The bike bounced over a couple of ruts in the road and came to rest about 50 yards from a large fire. Around the fire were men and women drinking and laughing. Some were lying on the ground while others fought with each other in drunken brawls.

I felt the bike pitch sideways as he pushed the kickstand down and leaned the bike heavily into it.

"Time to get off."

I dismounted as carefully as I could so as not to attract any attention to myself.

He reached around my shoulder and pulled me up against him and started walking towards the fire.

My feet and legs were numb as they marched without my will directing them towards the others.

As we approached, a man even larger than the one holding me looked up. He had been sitting on a log, his arm around a drunken woman. He watched for a second and then stood up and moved towards us.

Frozen and unable to stand the monster man held me up as the other approached.

"Who the hell are you and what did you bring him here for?" He snapped. "This isn't a party you just show up to, you need an invite."

The others had stopped the partying and were beginning to gather around us. It was obvious that whatever was going to happen was going to be great entertainment for them. I swallowed hard again. Apparently my friend didn't know these people and my first guess of him being an escapee from a mental institution rushed back into my mind.

"He's under my protection." The man holding me said in a booming voice that seemed to shake the ground itself."

"And who the hell are you that you're going to be protecting anyone?" The leader shot back taking a step forward.

"I think you are about to find out." The man holding me smiled back.

Oh my I thought, the guy is totally nuts and this is not going to be pretty. I felt like crying. The sounds and smells of the place were surreal and the hand on my shoulder threatened to squeeze right though me.

"What the hell did you say?" The leader sneered back and punched as fast a punch as I have ever seen.

I would have closed my eyes had I been able to but time seemed to slow to a crawl. I watched as if in slow motion as the punch moved out towards my handler and as quickly as it started it stopped. The punch just hung in mid air, only inches from the face of the man holding me.

The leader seemed to struggle, as if his hand was being held there. Finally it snapped back into his control and he almost fell as he pulled it back to his side.

"Cut that mother," he yelled and two men jumped forward pulling knives as they moved.

As soon as they stepped forward they too froze in space as if held by an invisible hand. Then they were picked up and thrown across the grass as if by some invisible force landing them in a heap.

The leader stared at the two of us. Obviously trying to piece together what had just happened.

"Thanks for participating in the demonstration. We'll be leaving now." My huge new friend said as he started to turn.

My handler then half carried and half pulled me back towards the bike.

It was at that second that I heard a sharp crack. I didn't know what it was for the first second but then realized it was a gunshot. I turned my head in time to see a man standing not more than ten feet away with a pistol pointed directly at us. I watched as a flame licked out of the muzzle and a second crack filled the air, then a third a forth and a fifth.

I was yanked back around towards the way we had come as two more loud cracks sounded yet I felt no pain, obviously I wasn't hit or if I was, I was in shock.

We mounted the bike and he kicked the starter and I watched in disbelief as three more gang members strode up to us firing pistols at us at almost point blank range.

The engine on the bike had roared into life and my big companion hit the throttle racing us along the road back towards the highway as swearing and more gunshots rang out behind us. On the back of the bike I flinched each time there was a sound, expecting to feel the hot pain of a bullet at any second.

When we hit the highway we turned back towards the bar and in minutes we were sitting back at the table.

I had checked myself at least four times for blood or wounds and found none. Looking at the man across from me I realized that he too seemed to have suffered no damage from what had happened.

As he ordered drinks for us I cautiously leaned forward and looked at him.

"What just happened back there and what if they come after us?"

"They won't," he answered and then he smiled. "So how did you like it?"

"Like what?" I managed to get out. I was starting to shake now as the true implications of what had happened started to sink in.

———

"Like finding out that I don't need anyone's protection."

"What!" I almost shouted across the table at him.

"I told you that I wanted you to experience what happened and that I would like you to let other people know."

Despite my shaking I was also starting to understand that something very strange was happening here right now.

"Don't you remember, just about an hour ago you asked me what I wanted you to do and I told you that I wanted you to experience something and tell people some things. Well what I want you to tell them is that I don't need looking after."

I tried to smile and nodded my head. It was obvious just looking at the man that under almost any circumstances he wouldn't need looking after but considering what I had just seen I was pretty sure that nothing I could think of could hurt him.

"Who or what are you?" I asked quietly. Our drinks had arrived and though I'm not what could be considered a drinker I downed a quarter of my beer almost in one gulp.

"I am an image of what you think is God." He answered. "I thought the beard would give me away." He smiled at me.

On hearing that I didn't know which was worse, what happened a few minutes ago or what was happening now.

"Think about it. You just were shot at, at point blank range by at least five people and you never got a scratch, nor did I. Doesn't that seem a bit strange to you?"

I nodded.

"Well the reason you didn't get a scratch is that I am an image of God and quite frankly I am pretty damn powerful." He sat back and smiled at his words.

My brain was unable to go anywhere with what he was saying. So the only option was to follow along.

"What do you mean the image of God? Do you mean that you're God?

"No, of course not, I'm just an image. You don't understand what God is yet, and that's one of my reasons for being here. To get you to understand what God is so you can experience God and tell other people about it. But before you can understand what I am talking about you need to understand that God doesn't need protection from anyone or anything. I'm trying to give this to you in small steps." He added, "And the first step is for you to understand that God does not need you or anyone else's protection."

I took another sip of my drink. My shaking was getting worse and I spilled a bit as I brought the glass to my mouth.

"Why would anyone think that God needed protection?" I asked.

"Because" he stated "Every major religion in the world right now believes that they have to protect God and because of that all their followers believe it too. Can you imagine a more stupid concept? There are Christians and Muslims that actually think that they need to enforce rules they attribute to God. They think that they need to punish people who break these imaginary rules and that God can be offended or hurt. These people, the so called religious have hijacked Gods teachings and actually believe and get others to believe that I can't take care of myself.

You've seen a small amount of what I can do. Did you know that I could cause a mountain to rise up and crush those bikers? If I had wanted I could stop this world from moving or instantly put a layer of ice ten miles thick over it.

Oh my I thought, this guy is so far gone I don't have words for it.

He gave me a very brief scowl, which made me think he somehow guessed what I was thinking and then continued.

Did you know that there are people being tortured in the Middle East right now because some whacko thought that God might be offended by what they did or said. Let me tell you, if God was offended He could easily do something about it himself. If I can stop bullets or make mountains rise do people really think that God needs them to prevent him from being insulted?"

He spoke as if he actually believed what he was saying. After a quick sip of his beer he continued.

"The same is true of many people in this country. They think they have to be the moral voice of what is right or wrong. They actually have the arrogance to think that they know what God wants to have happen? They, like you, can't even begin to understand what God is or what his purpose is, or what their purpose is for that matter." He smiled and his face softened for a moment as he finished his sentence.

He turned back to me as if I was some kind of employee that he was giving a job description.

"Your job is to simply let people know that God doesn't need protecting. Oh and a few other things that we all will get into a bit later on, but for now that is the start."

I was totally puzzled by what he said and though I was feeling a bit better I was convinced now that something very weird was going on. What that was I had no idea.

He seemed to ignore me and just continue with his telling me about God.

"Now to make sure you understand exactly what I have just told you means let me be very specific. If someone uses Gods name in vain or blasphemes God, God doesn't need any help protecting his name. If someone thinks that the blasphemer needs to be punished or hurt, that the perpetrator needs to be flogged or put to death for a sin they are totally wrong. God only creates and everything is a creation of God. Even the things people don't like at all!"

I was actually beginning to like what he was saying. Somehow it made sense to me at a deep level.

He carried on with what he seemed to think was the crowing glory of his talk.

——

"Any religion that has rules that cause people pain or cruelty is wrong. It doesn't matter if they are fundamentalist Christian or radical Muslim. If they think they are doing Gods will by telling other people how to behave or act they are dead wrong."

I sat stunned. The noise of the bar around me seemed to fade into the distance as I thought of what this man said. Either I was sitting talking to some kind of emissary from God or I was talking to a totally crazy person who seemed to have extraordinary powers.

"So what is it that God is exactly?" I questioned. "If you're not him, if you're an image does that mean you look like him or?" My sentence trailed off as I was unsure how to finish it.

"No I am not an image of how God is, I am an image of how God is to you. God is. Everything is God. There is nothing else. Everything that exists is God, be it a wife creating an omelet for her husband or a moviemaker creating a story for an audience God is what is. It's that simple."

"But I thought that God was all powerful and controlled what happened and such?"

"No" he answered abruptly. "You have long wondered if God actually even existed as have billions of others on your planet. You have wondered that because you didn't understand what God was. You thought of God as some kind of being that lived in the clouds or some spirit hovering around earth interfering with people. That is not what God is, or ever was. God simply is.

Everywhere in your world and beyond is creation. Every time you think you create. Every time you love or have an idea you create. All of that is God. God is everything and powerful and unstoppable. But unscrupulous people who want to wield power over others have hijacked his name. They do unthinkable things in the name of protecting something that needs no protection.

Does creation care if you don't believe in it? Of course not! Does creation care that you insult it? No. Creation does not care what your ideas or plans or thoughts are. Creation only cares that you create, that you uplift others and you make them feel good."

I finished my beer and felt a lot calmer. The shaking had stopped and I was ready to ask more questions but apparently he was finished for the evening.

"Well time for you to get some sleep." he mused and stood up.

"The bartender has your room ready. Just walk over to the bar and ask for the key. Oh and don't ever worry again. I will be with you and there is nothing that can hurt you once you really understand what is happening."

I stood up and stretched looking towards the bar. The bartender had reached under the counter and was holding a key in his hand as our eyes met.

As I turned back I couldn't believe my eyes. He was gone. I scoured the room for a moment trying to find him but he was nowhere to be seen. I could feel the panic rising again and was about to sit back down, my legs unable to hold me when I felt his hand on my shoulder again.

—

"Remember, I am always here, you just don't see me most of the time". His voice filled my head and then the hand was gone.

I walked to the bar and took the key, then walked out of the door and back to the motel.

When I woke the next morning I wasn't sure if it all had been a dream or not, after all, how could it have been true. I had been so tired I was sure I had dreamed it.

I got showered and dressed and stepped out into a beautiful day. The bar was closed and all the bikes save one were gone. It looked vaguely like the one he had rode. My curiosity was such that I couldn't leave without taking a closer look.

As I approached the bike I recognized it as the one in my dream. I reached down and touched it. It was then that I noticed the small round holes in the muffler.

I straightened up suddenly feeling very strange and noticed that sticking out from under the seat was a letter. I looked around and then reached down and pulled it out. It had my name nicely written in large letters and was sealed. I opened it and inside was a folded piece of paper, an ignition key and the ownership certificate for the motorcycle made out to me.

I flipped open the folded page. In the same handwritten text as the name on the front of the letter a simple message was left. It read

"THE BIKE IS YOURS NOW AS A REMINDER OF WHAT GOD IS AND THAT YOU HAVE GOD WITHIN YOU. ALL YOU NEED TO DO NOW IS LEARN THAT ANY MISUNDERSTANDINGS ARE YOUR'S.

AS FOR YOUR OTHER QUESTIONS YOU HAVE A CHOICE. YOU CAN RETURN TO YOUR CAR AND CONTINUE YOUR JOURNEY AND YOUR LIFE…OR YOU CAN GET ON THE BIKE AND LET IT LEAD YOU DOWN A NEW ROAD. ONE THAT WHEN FOLLOWED WILL ANSWER THE QUESTIONS YOU ASKED LAST NIGHT AND MORE.

SIGNED

AIG (An Image of God).

PS. ALL CREATION IS OF AND FROM GOD. YOU CREATE NOTHING ALONE AND BECAUSE OF THAT YOU ARE ALWAYS PART OF EVERYTHING.

ENJOY THE RIDE IF YOU CHOOSE TO TAKE IT.

Chapter Three

The note sat on my passenger seat as I pulled out of the parking lot and turned to take one last look at the bike. I couldn't just leave everything, I didn't have enough money or even know what I would tell people. I was on a short trip, just to clear my mind. My job hadn't been going so well, my relationship was over and I needed time I had thought, a bit of the open road to get my mind clear.

I pulled out onto the main road and begin to accelerate when something in the ditch caught my eye. It was yellow, or at least it looked yellow.

Stepping on the brake I steered for the shoulder pulled the car to a stop while asking myself what the heck I was doing. I had enough on my plate without inviting more into my life.

As I got out of the car to investigate I heard a wonderful melodic voice sing out to me.

"Hi there, I was wondering if anyone would stop?"

Sitting in the ditch was a delightful looking woman wearing a halter-top and shorts. The most amazing thing though was that she was sporting a bright yellow cast that she had supported on a branch to keep her leg in the air. The cast went from the bottom of her shorts to her foot.

"My gosh, what are you doing out here?" I yelled back.

"Waiting for you to pick me up. I have to get to the next town, would you mind giving me a lift?"

I nodded in disbelief as she unhooked herself from the branch that was supporting her leg and began to struggle to stand up.

"Have to keep my leg up when I can." She laughed.

I ran over to help her stand and together we hobbled back to my car, where the real problems started.

Try as we could she simply could not get into either the back or front of my car. With her leg sticking straight out because of the cast and my car being on the smaller side it was impossible to get her into the vehicle.

"Too bad you don't have a motorcycle." She cooed. "That's how I got this far. I just put my foot up on the front foot rest and I'm set to go."

I thought for a second and the decision became crystal clear. I would go back and get the bike, take her to the next town and then come back for my car.

"Can you wait here for a couple of minutes? I have a bike back at the motel."

Instead of being surprised that I would have a motorcycle handy she just smiled.

"Sure" she said and started to sit down again on the side of the road as I ran around to the driver side and hopped in my car.

A few minutes later we were both sailing effortlessly down the highway, the hot wind blowing in my face and her arms wrapped around me. I couldn't think of a better place to be this wonderful morning.

The bike seemed built for me as we navigated the winding road and I felt more at home than I had felt for a long long time. Perhaps that strange biker was right. I needed to take this bike for a ride and I needed to change my life. It was certainly not what I would have thought that I wanted when I started out, but I was enjoying it, a lot. I really didn't know how I could have gotten so off track but now, here I was, the wind in my face, a beautiful woman holding me tight and the deep rumble of the engine under me. If it hadn't started to rain things would have been perfect.

As the first raindrops hit me I thought that perhaps I had driven into something that birds leave behind from time to time but when the sky began darkening and the drops continued to come I knew we were in for a downpour.

"I hate to tell you this but I really shouldn't get my cast wet" She yelled in my ear.

"No problem, I'm looking for a place to stop." I yelled back over the roar of the engine.

"What about over there?" She pointed to what appeared to be an abandoned house sitting back from the side of the road.

"Any port in a storm" I yelled back as I slowly applied the breaks and backed off on the throttle.

A minute or two later we were bumping over the dirt road towards the falling down house. The rain was causing small dust clouds to rise up around us each time a raindrop hit the road.

I pulled the bike under the porch and put the kickstand down, testing to make sure the old wood would hold it. It held fine and I slipped my leg off the bike and began helping her to her feet. There was an old swing sitting on the porch and we both sat back on it as the sound of the rain above us started in earnest.

"I don't know if we should go inside, the floor may not be too solid" I said.

"She just nodded and huddled closer to me. The temperature was dropping rapidly with the rain and like it or not we were probably going to have to go inside or freeze out here. I was not dressed for riding and she was wearing less than me.

For now though I was content to let her cuddle against me as we watched the darkening sky and listened to the music of the rain above us.

Chapter Four

I had pushed the door open and done a bit of exploring inside. The floor seemed fine, in fact it seemed almost too good considering the age and look of the outside of the house.

I arranged a couple of old bits of wood to sit on when I heard a sound and looked up. It was her and she was carrying the saddlebags from the bike.

"Looks like you come prepared at least." She chuckled.

I looked in amazement as she pulled a jacket that seemed made for me out of the saddlebags and a second one that fit her nicely, if a tiny bit big. There was also a blanket and two fold up chairs with legs that stretched out and then were tightened with small hand tightened screws.

"Why didn't you tell me you had a couple of jackets?" she asked as I pulled the zipper up feeling the warmth surround me.

"I well, actually didn't know." She just nodded and smiled and sat down beside me on the fold up chair and we looked through the broken window watching the rain.

Within half an hour or so the rain had passed and the temperature was rising again, so I got up and looked out the door to survey the road. It hadn't rained long but it had been a real downpour. The dirt road looked pretty bad and I wasn't sure I could make it out until it dried a bit.

As if she had been reading my thoughts she put her hand on my shoulder. I turned around as she smiled. "We can wait for the sun to dry the road. Shouldn't take more than an hour or so and we can use the time to get to know each other."

Sitting on the porch in the warm sun we talked for the next hour or so. I explained how I had been on the road and what had happened in my life. How my job was pretty dull and I had just felt that I needed to get away. I also did my best to explain about the bike and how I came to have it, feeling a bit sheepish as I talked about how the guy had told me he was a messenger from God.

"Did he actually tell you he was a messenger from God?" She asked.

"Well no, not exactly", I answered; he told me he was an AIG, an image of God.

"Wow, so if you hadn't seen me on the side of the road you would have left the bike?"

I mused over her question for a moment before answering. "Yea, I guess I would have."

"So I suppose that makes me part of this plan for you to start down a new road."

I laughed a bit but she was right. If she hadn't been there or if I had been able to get her leg into the car the bike would still be sitting at the motel.

We were both quiet for a bit and then she spoke up.

"Do you think I'm an AIG too?"

I looked over at her and I wanted to tell her that as far as I was concerned she certainly was but somehow the words didn't quite make it out of my mouth. I just nodded and smiled.

"You are beautiful" I said and then turned away, embarrassed at my words somehow.

The road was fairly dry now, at least dry enough to ride through and by staying on the grass at the side of the road I easily made it to the main highway and we were on our way again.

The next town appeared far too soon for me and as we motored down the main street she pointed to a side street and I nosed the bike around the corner.

At the end of the block was a small house with a huge yard.

"That's where I'm going. My Aunt lives there and I need to see her. She called me and she's quite ill."

She had not told me that before and somehow her coming to nurse her sick Aunt hadn't crossed my mind. I pulled up in front of the house and she hobbled off the bike and removed the jacket.

"Thank you so much for the ride. I know you made the right decision." She leaned over and kissed my softly on the cheek and then was hobbling down the path to the front door before I had even got off the bike.

I was thinking about getting off the bike but her Aunt was already at the door and holding out her arms to greet her niece. I somehow felt out of place, an outsider and though I was sure I would have been welcomed I wanted to leave. This was somehow not where I was comfortable. I twisted around and put the jacket back in the saddlebag and then looked at the two of them.

The Aunt looked up at me as she hugged her niece and nodded to me. I nodded back and hit the start button. The bike roared to life and I turned back along the street towards the main part of town. I wanted to look into the mirror but I chose to keep my eyes on the road ahead.

About two blocks down there was a park so I decided that I would just pull in there for a bit and think. I needed to decide if I was going to head back for the car or just leave it there for a bit. When I had picked up the motorcycle I had knocked on the motel door and the bartender had answered. I had explained the situation and he seemed totally fine with the whole thing, no questions and had even suggested that I put the car around the back. He said that he would look after it for me and that I need not worry. He told me that travelers sometimes left things for him to take care of and they always got them back just as they had left them. Then he added, if they wanted them.

I hadn't thought much about his words due to my rush to get back to the woman with the cast but it struck me as kind of weird as I thought about it now. Oh well, I justified to myself. I had nothing of value in the car and the bike was probably worth two or three times what the car was worth so even if they stripped my car and sold it I was still ahead.

I lay down on the grass in the sun beside the bike and looked up at the sky. I didn't think I should be tired but somehow I just felt very relaxed and as I gazed up at the blue sky sprinkled with bright white clouds I was beginning to believe that last night was real. I knew rationally it couldn't be, but deep down inside it was becoming very real to me somehow.

I shut my eyes and the biker was back in front of me.

"Remember God doesn't need your protection. Any religion that says he does is totally wacko." He laughed and I started awake. The park was still there and the sky still blue. It was a dream I thought as I sat up and looked around.

I was suddenly aware that I was hungry, really hungry and that I should take a look around for a place to eat.

Straddling the bike I headed back down the main street and pulled into a smallish but nice looking cafe. Inside I sat down and ordered the special.

The waitress brought the special a few minutes later and poured me a cup of coffee. As she moved away I saw a big poster on the bulletin board. It was advertising an evangelical tent service later that evening. As I ate I thought that it was about time that I got a bit better idea about religion and what was being said about God.

Chapter Five

The preacher was great. He spoke well and paced up and down like a panther tracking his pray.

He led the audience on a roller coaster ride of emotions. From tears to rejoicing and at the end, the line up for "saving" was long. He had obviously done a good job as at least half the people in the huge tent, maybe more, had decided to step up and be saved.

I had enjoyed it but there were some nagging questions in a lot of what he had said. He had told us all that God needed us to stand tall and to preach his message. He was pretty direct about it telling us in a lot of different ways that God wanted us to do his bidding or he would be very angry.

I stayed until the end and then asked if I could have a minute of the pastor's time. I explained that I had driven a long way to hear him and reluctantly the helper led me to a huge motor home behind the tent and knocked on the door.

A moment later the minister answered and I was sitting at a small table being offered a cup of tea.

"So what is so urgent that you need to speak to me right now, I am a bit tired after the service." His eyes glazed a bit for a moment and then returned to me.

"Well Sir, I have basically one question to ask you."

"Ask away." He replied as he sipped his tea.

"Do you believe that God needs us to look after him, you know to defend his truths and his teachings?"

Without batting an eye he answered. "Yes of course. God wants us to defend the faith. He wants us to do everything we can to spread the word and to defend our beliefs against those heathens that would destroy our way of life and our religion."

"But if God is so powerful, why doesn't he just look after himself?"

The pastor eyed me with a new scrutiny. "Who sent you boy? What are you really asking?"

"No one sent me, I just wanted to know why, if God is so all powerful he needs us to fight his wars or tell people about him, why can't he do it himself?"

"God is a spirit, he doesn't do things himself. He waits for us to do them and if we do them the way he wants then he rewards us, and if we fail to do them he punishes us. Its that simple boy." He leaned back in his chair but never took his eyes off me.

"You didn't answer my question Sir. If he is all powerful why would he need us to fight for him or to do anything for him for that matter?"

"You just don't get it boy." He answered. "Our job is to do Gods bidding for him, not the other way around."

"Then why pray, why ask God to do things for us if he won't?"

"Sometimes he does boy, as I said, you just don't get it. If we do enough for him, if we pray and are his people in mind and body then he will reward us by giving us his blessings."

"So its kind of like a trade off." I said.

"If that's the way you want to see it I suppose that is one way of looking at it." He laughed a bit as he said this and then started to stand.

"Well if there is nothing more I can do for you I really do have a lot to do and it's been a very busy evening." He held his hand out towards the door.

As I walked back towards the bike I couldn't quite get his words to jive with what I had been told by the AIG. But the minister made sense. It was what I had been taught.

As I rode towards the lights of town I wondered what exactly was right. Did we need to fight God's fights, to stand up for him and make him right in the face of people disbelieving in him or having a different religion?

There was a bright motel sign at the end of the street and I figured it was time for me to rest.

The room wasn't that fancy but it was clean and I fell into a deep sleep as soon as I hit the pillow.

In my dreams I was back on the bike again with the AIG. I saw the pistols firing point blank and felt the fear and a strange kind of security. I hadn't noticed the secure feeling before, there was so much happening and then I was awake in the dark room. Starring at the ceiling and unable to sleep, the bikers words going through my head.

——

The knock at the door startled me fully awake. I listened, not sure if it was my dream or a real knock. It came again, a muffled knock at my door.

Throwing back the covers I sleepily moved to the door and squinted though he peephole. It was her. She was standing out side my room. I checked my watch…3:30 in the morning.

"Just a minute, I have to put some pants on." I called through the door as I fumbled with my jeans.

A moment later I threw open the door and in she walked. Stunned I stood there for a moment and I'm sure I had my mouth open. She was wearing the exact same things she had been wearing yesterday except the bright yellow cast was gone.

She closed the door behind her and walked to the only chair in the room and sat down. I must have looked a scene as she smiled at me and motioned for me to sit on the bed.

"I suppose you weren't expecting me?"

I managed to close my mouth and move over to the bed and sit down.

"What happened to your cast? Did you just get it off today?"

"It comes and goes as need be." She answered with a smile.

Trying to get my mind to work I asked her what she was doing here at this time of the night. It didn't come out sounding very welcoming but it was the best I could do.

"You need to visit someone tomorrow and you will need an early start to get there."

"What do you mean I need to visit someone tomorrow? What are you talking about and why are you telling me this now?" I wanted her to stay but I was feeling very confused.

"I also am an AIG," she smiled, "and I'm here to get you to your next destination."

Suddenly the loss of her cast made a lot of sense. If she was another of these "images of God" angel types then she could get rid of a cast anytime she wanted.

"So it was a set up then?" I asked.

"I suppose you could call it that, but if I hadn't been there you would have driven right past and we didn't want that. I wanted you to stop and besides, you had a great day yesterday didn't you? Wasn't it fun being free instead of stuck inside those confining beliefs you would have kept had you continued in your car?"

She was right. It was fun. I had found myself enjoying my life more yesterday than I had for a long time.

"So do you want to know where you are going this morning?" she smiled.

"Sure, why not let me know where you want me to go this morning."

"Then turn on the TV and find out."

"OK if that's the game." I turned around and reached for the remote and waited for a couple of seconds for the TV screen to brighten.

—

"Any particular channel or is this just God TV?" I asked with a smirk.

"No this one will do nicely. Now we just have to wait for the news."

"Oh." I replied and sat back against the headboard of the bed.

"So how long have you been an angel?" I asked.

"I'm not an angel." She responded. "I'm an AIG."

"Yea, yea." I replied. "You look a lot like an angel to me, especially when you show up at three thirty in the morning on my doorstep."

"You're lucky I'm not an angel," she laughed. "Angels I'm sure would take offense at your thoughts right now."

"And you?" I chided.

"Me? It's flattering, but we do have business and you are a bit young for me."

"Young, well I won't ask you your age then, I know that's not polite." I smiled back at her. Inside though I felt less than happy. It was very obvious now that she had not even the slightest interest in me as a man and quite frankly it hurt my ego. Not that I had any false ideas about my looks or stature. I was what I was but still, I had enjoyed the moments with her. Especially when we cuddled against the cold and rain. My mind was jarred back to the hotel room by the T.V. announcer telling us that after the commercial break the news would be right up.

"This what we are waiting for?" I asked.

She nodded and we both turned back to the T.V.

A couple of minutes later a dark man wearing what appeared to be a spotted cloth or hood of some type on his head and sporting a dark beard was on the screen. He was telling a group of people that he would be giving a talk that evening to let all the people know that we should be allowing Sharia Law be practiced in this country. He went on to say that it was about time that the true believers be allowed to practice what is the true law as put forth by his religion and that he would be holding an information news conference later that evening.

He ranted for a few more seconds about Islam and then the screen blinked to a couple of football players talking stats for the last game.

"Is that what you wanted me to see?" I asked.

She nodded.

"So what I am supposed to do with that guy. He looks like a crackpot to me."

"He is actually," she smiled. "But he is a crack pot that is important to your journey.

"OK. So lets say I go see this guy I don't even know where he is or how to find him. Do I just sit here and see him this evening?"

"Oh no, if it was that easy I would have come to see you at a more reasonable hour. You are going to have to go see him this morning. He lives in the Capital, just a couple of hours from here. I will draw you a map to get to his place."

—

"OK, so I go to his place. Then what? What the heck am I supposed to do, just walk up and ring his doorbell?"

"That sounds like a great idea."

I leaned back against the headboard. "And what if I don't want to ride for two hours this morning to go see this moron?"

Then you will understand less than you wanted to understand. The journey you wanted to take will be lessoned and you won't learn what you want to learn.

"And just what is it that I want to learn so badly?"

"You want to learn the truth. You have always wanted to know the truth, to understand why you were put here and what your purpose is, or if you even have a purpose. You want to know why there is suffering in the world and you want to know if there really is a God. And most importantly you want to know what you are."

"And going to see this guy is going to answer these questions?"

"It's a start." She smiled back at me. "Well I have to go. The map is on your table over there."

I looked and sure enough there was a paper sitting there I hadn't seen before.

"Do you people enjoy this?" I asked as she stood.

"Actually we do." she answered as she moved towards the door.

"It will take you about two and half hours to get there and then another half hour to make it through the city to his place. I would hop in the shower if I were you. Especially if you're going to be there before he leaves for his first appointment."

The door shut behind her and she was gone. It was almost as if she hadn't been there at all. I had the same weird feeling I had when I met the fellow who gave me his bike. Why don't they give me their names I thought? It's really confusing not to know who they are.

Twenty minutes later the cold night air was rushing against my face as I made my way down the main street heading for the highway turnoff.

Chapter Six

It had been a very refreshing ride. The cold morning air kept me awake as I cruised along the road. I had been doing a lot of thinking too. I wasn't sure what I was supposed to say or do or learn. I didn't know why I was doing this and yet here I was, cold and hungry barreling down the highway to go see a man I only learned existed a few hours ago.

I noticed my turn off and applied the brakes, leaned the bike into the turn and twisted the throttle again. The noise of the engine against the early morning sunrise reverberated in the residential neighborhood and I half expected pajama-clad residents to appear at their doorways waving their fists and shouting obscenities for my waking them.

I counted off the blocks and then there it was. His street. I throttled back, the reality of actually going up to his door upon me. Cruising slowly down the street I arrived at the right number.

The house was not as big as I had imagined. It was a small single story rancher with a nice looking front yard. Good resale value I mused as I turned into the driveway and shut down the engine, coasting the last four or five feet.

The lights were on so I knew they were awake. I was pretty sure they had heard the bike and was half expecting them to come running out wondering how or what had appeared in their driveway at 7:00 or so in the morning.

I flipped the kickstand down and waited. No one at the door and no sounds, I guess they were used to strange bikes riding up their driveway.

There was nothing to do but go up to the door and ring the bell. I had no idea what I would say as I took the last couple of steps towards the door. Standing in the dark I reached over to the glowing doorbell and pressed it once and then stepped back.

A moment later a kindly looking older woman came to the door and opened it a crack.

"Hi there," I stuttered. "I'm here to see.."

My sentence was cut short by her slamming the door in my face.

Well that worked out really well, I thought to myself as I turned to go when I heard the door open again. I turned back and there was the man himself.

"What can I do for you at this time in the morning?" was his curt question.

I didn't blame him. If some strange guy on a bike had shown up at my place at seven in the morning I wouldn't be too happy either.

"I came to talk to you, to ask you a couple of questions…about God." I had no idea what to say and was embarrassed by what had come out of my mouth.

"And what if the answers you get are not what you are seeking?" He replied back.

—

"I suppose I will have to live with them." I answered.

My gosh this sounds like some B movie script I thought to myself as I waited for his answer.

"Then come in. Allah must have sent you because no infidel would show up at my door speaking such things unless Allah was behind it."

He pushed the door open and motioned for me to come in.

I entered his house and removed my shoes and we moved to his kitchen where he offered me a Turkish coffee.

"It is quite strong," he laughed as the older lady busied herself in preparing it.

I nodded and thanked him.

"So Mr...", his sentence trailed off waiting for me to introduce myself. I told him my name and he continued.

"What can I do for you? It is obvious you have ridden a ways to get here and so you must have something important to tell me."

"Actually it is ask you, not tell you?" I answered.

"But before I ask my questions, I want to thank you for your hospitality. I really didn't expect such kindness."

"From an extremist?" He put in at the end of my sentence.

"Actually I didn't say that, but you do sound quite committed to your views from what you said on the TV this morning."

"Before we go further, let me introduce you to my brothers." He motioned with his hand and three men stepped forward from the shadows of the darkened rooms leading off the kitchen. Each of them was carrying what appeared to be a small machine gun.

My heart stopped and I started to stand and then sat back down heavily.

"Don't worry my friend, we will not hurt you. I just wanted you to know that I am not so unprotected and trusting as you might believe. Had you made any threatening moves towards me you would have already been dead."

"Well I can assure you that I have no hostile reasons for being here." I sputtered

"Yes, we felt that was the case or you would not still be sitting here." He smiled, as did his gun-toting friends. "I hope you don't mind them joining us?"

"Not at all." I answered looking back and forth at them.

"So, lets have our coffee and get down to business. What exactly can I do for you? What do you want to know?"

"Well, I don't know if you'll believe this or not, but I had a visit from a kind of emissary…" I realized how bizarre this was sounding as I heard the words coming out of my mouth, "…from God I think?"

All four men started to laugh.

"So you are telling us that God has talked to you and now you come to see me?"

—

"Well in a manner of speaking." I answered.

"Then I was right, Allah has led you to us." He smiled at his own humour.

"Well actually it wasn't like that exactly," I looked around at the men and the guns and suddenly felt very stupid. "I came to ask you a couple of questions."

"Then ask."

"Why do you think God needs protecting?" I managed to get out. It was the only question that came to mind and it reflected back exactly on what the first AIG had said.

"What do you mean God needing protection? Allah is all powerful, he needs nothing."

"Then if he needs nothings why do you believe that it is wrong for someone to criticize your religion, or for that matter to not be part of your religion?"

He looked at me long and hard for a moment and then smiled. "You have asked a question that is blasphemous. You are unaware of the power of God, he instructs us to do his bidding and we are but his pawns. We have no choice but to follow our destiny, the path he has set out for us."

His answer was double talk and I realized that he was trying to intimidate me. Something that the guns had already done very well, but I was already here and I wanted to understand if he really got my question at all?"

"You don't understand. If God is so powerful why does he need you to enforce any rules or laws? Don't you think he's big and strong enough to look after people he doesn't like himself?"

The man was beginning to get angry. I could see it in his eyes even though he masked it with a false smile.

"Spoken like an infidel who knows nothing of God or of the Koran. God has told us what to do and how to do it. He tells us how to live and how to pray and what we must do. It is you and people like you that don't understand. God is everywhere and almighty."

It was obvious that he didn't get the question or didn't want to understand it. I listened in an almost detached place as he quoted verses from the Koran and told me how God had ordained the followers of Islam to do and act in certain ways. The AIG's words formed the backdrop as I listened. If God was so powerful and had so many powers why would he want to have powerless humans doing his dirty work? What difference to God would it make if someone believed in a different religion. If God didn't like something or wanted to change it he could with the wave of his hand.

I interrupted the outpouring of verses with a second question.

"If God wants everyone to be Muslims why doesn't he just make it so?"

"Because you must choose to follow his wishes. You must choose the path of Islam."

"But if God controls your destiny, and thus your life then that means he controls what you believe and if you actually come to believe in your religion. So if a person doesn't believe in Islam then God has caused the person to not believe in Islam."

The man stood and shouted something in a language I didn't understand to the men standing around us. They moved closer to me. I stood understanding that it was time to go.

"You insult Islam and you insult me. I have invited you into my house and offered you my hospitality and this is how you repay me. By insulting my Religion?"

I was angry. I was tired of being given such stupid answers to what were becoming very real questions. "If Allah is so powerful then I am sure he doesn't need you and your gun toting henchmen to look after him." I taunted.

A moment later I was on the front lawn.

"You are lucky you are not in my country" he yelled red faced from the door, "I would have your throat cut for your blasphemy."

I was angry, so angry in fact I could hardly remember feeling so frustrated and mad. I shouted back at him. "If this is not your country then get the hell out and go back to where you belong." He slammed the door. I could see the silhouette of the men in the darkness of the open windows as I moved to my bike and hit the start button.

A moment later I felt a freedom I had not often felt as I put distance between a very crazy and dangerous man and myself.

I drove for about ten minutes and saw a small restaurant in the next block. I was shaking and needed to get off the bike and just sit for a few minutes. I pulled into the parking lot and in a couple of minutes was sitting in a soft warm booth sipping a regular coffee as best I could. My hands still shook and I felt exhausted. My God, that man is beyond reason I thought as I gazed out into the morning rush hour.

"So are you ready to order?"

The plump older waitress was standing there watching me intently.

"I uh, haven't looked at the menu yet."

She turned her head and looked around the diner as if to make sure it was OK for her to be there with me and then sat down across from me.

"He got to you didn't he?"

I blinked and stared into her face.

"What?"

"He got to you didn't he, kind of scared you? He scares us too and its not just him, it's the whole idea that he and the rest of them are pushing. The idea that God can't take care of himself and that he needs self-righteous thugs to threaten people into believing. What a pile of horse hockey." She paused for a moment. "I'll give you a moment more, but I would order the scrambled with bacon. Best in the city and it'll warm you up on the inside too."

She stood and walked back to the counter, picked up a coffee pot and headed off to look after another table.

—

I sat in a kind of shock watching her. How many of them are there I thought.

A couple of minutes later she returned.

"I put in the order for scrambled for you, figured it was the least we could do. I'm off in about twenty so how about we talk for a few minutes when I get off shift. You'll enjoy the eggs, they are the best in the city, no lie."

She walked across the floor and disappeared into the kitchen. A few minutes later she reappeared with the scrambled eggs and placed them in front of me, refilled my coffee cup and walked away without a word.

She was right, the eggs were fantastic, or maybe it was just my hunger. Being scared shitless really works up an appetite I was beginning learn.

I was sitting with my plate pushed to the side nursing my coffee when she reappeared.

"So how were the eggs? Good don't you think?"

I nodded as she sat down.

"So I guess you figured out who I am?" she asked as she straightened her dress.

"I would suppose that you are another one of those AIG's that keep visiting me like Christmas ghosts."

She laughed and smiled broadly. "I like that, Christmas ghosts."

"So what is it that you are going to tell me to do?"

"Nothing at all," she answered, "I'm kind of a de-briefer. Just here to talk for a bit."

"Oh."

"So what did you think of our friend?" She asked as another waitress brought her a coffee, the other waitress looked at me and then winked at my companion.

"He was scary, really scary?" I answered.

"And why was that exactly?"

"Well for the first thing he had guys with guns and believe it or not that scares me plenty."

"And…"

"Well the way he believed so strongly that he was right and…"

"It wasn't that he had put himself in charge of what other people should do?"

"Yea, that's what I meant I suppose. He felt he had a right to tell other people what they should be doing."

"Well it shouldn't surprise you when he figures he has a right to tell God what to do."

"What do you mean tell God what to do?"

"Well didn't you listen to what he told you? Didn't you get the whole idea that he was telling everyone that God wanted him to do all those things he talked about?"

"Well yea, but I don't recall him saying he was telling God to do anything."

"Didn't he say God was going to help him and God was on his side and all the rest?"

I nodded.

"Well do you really think that God is going to do all of that? Especially when the guy is out to lunch anyway."

"Well I thought that he was telling me what he believed God wanted him to say."

"Are you defending him?" She smiled as she asked the question.

"Well no." I realized that it had sounded very much like I was.

"The problem is that he is using subtle manipulation on his followers. When he tells them what God will and will not do he puts into their minds an image of what God is and it is totally incorrect."

She leaned forward as if to tell me a secret.

"God tries to help people get what they want, but it's insulting when they want him to act like an asshole to other people. As you have been told before tonight he doesn't need anyone defending him and he certainly doesn't need anyone telling anyone else what he likes or dislikes. Imagine the nerve."

She sat back and reached for her coffee shaking her head. Then she leaned forward again still obviously perturbed.

"Can you get over the nerve of some people? First telling every one around them what God is thinking and what he wants them to do and then to top it all making up rules as to what God is. Then they top it all off by deciding that they are going to be in charge of enforcing the lies they tell. It's enough to make any deity a bit hot under the collar."

She sat back and seemed to have said her piece.

"So what has that got to do with me? If God's so unhappy why the heck doesn't he do something about it? Especially considering that you are telling me he can."

She looked through me, her eyes darkening. "Who says he isn't."

The twinkle returned to her eyes and she stretched her arms over her head. "Well time to head off, it's been a long night and I need to get a bit of shut eye. Have a split shift today and let me tell you, it can tire a body out."

She stood up and started to leave and then stopped and turned back towards the table.

"You know, if I were you I would take that new route south. I hear it's a great road for a bike and who knows, you might meet some very interesting people down that way."

With that she turned and walked to the door and was gone.

Chapter Seven

I decided to take her advice and turned south as I headed out of town. The sun was warm and the traffic was light. I was glad to see the last of the city and was looking forward to a few hours of nothing but the open road and the sun.

A bit after twelve I pulled into a small rest stop. After using the bathroom I sat on the grass beside the bike for a while just soaking up the sun and thinking when I noticed a young boy standing looking in my direction.

He was about ten I would have guessed and he seemed very interested in my bike.

"So do you like it?" I asked.

He wasn't paying any attention to me and jumped when I spoke.

"Yea mister, great bike, what you pay for it?"

I smiled. "Not a thing, it was a gift."

"No kidding, wow, you must have rich friends mister."

I could hear his mother calling in the distance. "Is she calling you? I think she wants you to go."

"Yea, she does," he quipped back as he continued to ogle the bike. "I don't listen a lot though, at least that's what she tells me."

"Maybe you should listen this time."

He looked up at me and hesitated for a second and then ran off. I hadn't even noticed the fat guy sit down in the lawn chair about two feet from where I was.

"Bet you thought that he was one of us right?"

I spun my head around and looked the guy over. He was about five foot nothing and must have weighed at least three hundred pounds. The chair looked like it was going to collapse and my first thought was to move further away so he didn't roll on to me when the chair broke.

"So I guess you're my next Christmas ghost?"

He smiled and leaned over towards me bending the legs of the chair precariously, "You could say that, if it was Christmas."

He sat back upright and I breathed a silent sigh of relief.

"You don't like fat people do you?"

"What, what do you mean?"

"I mean just what I said. Since I got here most of what you have been thinking about was stupid stuff about me falling out of the chair and rolling on to you or you being crushed by me or some other dumb things."

"Its not that I don't like fat people…" I didn't know exactly what to say and figured that silence would be the best.

He smiled broadly and started laughing. "Got you on that one didn't I." He laughed so hard that I was again afraid he would tip and crush the life out of me.

—

After what seemed an eternity he got control of himself again and except for the occasional chuckle seemed to be serious.

"So what do you think a fat guy can teach you?"

I already knew he knew I had no idea so I just shrugged.

He looked up and gestured with his eyes for me to look.

"Hey, that kid is coming back again."

Sure enough the kid was back, this time with another slightly older boy. Probably his brother I thought as the two of them approached.

"Take a look at this bike will ya, that guy there," the boy nodded towards me, "told me a friend of his gave it to him." The other boy nodded and both of them stared at the bike.

The fat guy stood up and waddled over to them. "So you two like bikes?"

They both nodded. "How would you like it if I took you both for a spin."

All three of us looked shocked for a second but it was the older boy that spoke first.

"Hey mister, that's not your bike is it?"

"No but I think you need a ride and I figure I should take you for one."

By this time the father was on his way over, probably to collect the kids.

The fat guy reached down and grabbed one of the boys by the arm and started to lift him up. The boy started screaming and the father broke into a run to get to his son. I was on my feet when the father grabbed the boys other arm and started to pull. The man was yelling for the fat man to let go of his son but the fat man totally ignored him.

"Let him go you fat bastard," the father screamed as he punched at the fat man.

In what I would have considered an impossible feat the fat man seemed to move like lightening and easily avoided the punch and using his weight pushed the father back.

I heard a second voice yelling. "What the hell do you think you're doing" and realized the voice was mine. I was on my feet and moving around the bike to face the fat man too.

I towered over him but wasn't sure exactly what to do.

"I'd hit me if I were you." He whispered to me with a wink.

"What, what the hell are you doing?"

"You don't listen very well do you," he mumbled as he stepped forward towards me still holding the struggling boy with one hand.

He swung his free arm around at me and I ducked under it. By this time the boys' father was again trying to hit or grab the fat man.

Like a cat he eluded the fathers attempts to touch him and with a push sent the father flying backwards and landing on the grass behind us.

—

"What the hell are you doing" I screamed and rushed forward catching the fat man by the throat. I pushed backward and to my amazement he seemed to weigh nothing and went sailing across the parking lot, sending the boy sprawling.

The fat man stood up and shook himself off, looked directly at me and held up his hands as if to ward me off.

"OK, OK, that's enough tough guy, I'm gone." He turned and ran as fast as he could towards a dark blue car sitting a couple of parking places down from my bike.

The father by this time was by his son's side checking him for injuries as the fat man was leaping into his car. The side window was down and I'm sure no one but me saw the fat guy wink at me as he drove out of the parking lot.

A moment later the young boys mother was at my side.

"How can we thank you. I don't know what we would have done if you hadn't been there."

I turned and looked at her numbly. "Sure, uh, anyone would have helped if they could have."

The father was now beside me and passed the crying child over to his mother. He held out his hand.

"Thanks mister, I owe you."

I nodded and again made some remark about anyone helping in a situation like this.

"We have the police on the way, do you mind waiting?" The mother was talking to me but I was having a hard time listening I was shaking so hard.

"I don't know what I can add, I have no idea who that guy was or what he was up to." I answered.

"Oh we understand that, we just felt that you deserved some recognition for what you did, especially the way you handled yourself with that monster."

I followed the three of them over to their camper and sat down still shaking from head to toe.

"So you a martial artist?' The father asked.

"Me, no, not really. Took a few lessons a few years back but, no." I answered.

"Well you must have been one tough guy when you were in practice then." The father sheepishly laughed as he spoke. "That asshole was one fast guy. I can't believe he could move like that, and the way you moved, that was unbelievable. If I hadn't seen it I wouldn't have believed it possible."

I turned and looked at him.

The boy had quieted down and was sitting quietly sobbing with his mother holding him.

"I haven't seen anyone move that fast in my life, and I was in the army and we had some pretty tough cookies. The way you moved and threw that guy was unreal. Thank God you were here when you were. I couldn't have stopped him and he would have gotten Gord. You saved his life you know."

—

I knew I was sounding like I was trying to be modest but for the life of me I couldn't understand what had happened. As far as I could remember I hadn't moved fast and the guy weighed nothing. It was like pushing a cream puff.

"I really didn't do anything much." I replied.

About ten minutes went by and then we all heard the sirens wailing in the distance and I knew it would be only seconds before the police were here.

After taking names and particulars and talking at length to the family an older officer came over to me.

"These don't usually end up with happy endings. I'm glad that you were here and you can bet that the family over there is too. I don't often say this but thanks for getting involved."

I nodded and he moved to his car and I could hear him talking on the radio.

I was sitting on my bike. Not sure exactly what I should be doing and staring off into space when the first young boy tugged at my pants. I looked down and smiled.

"Thanks mister." He said, "you saved my brothers life." He then turned and walked back towards his family and the crowd that had gathered around their camper.

"So how's it feel to be a savior?"

I snapped my head around and there was the fat man, but somehow he looked like he had lost at least two hundred pounds.

"What the hell is happening here?" I snarled at him.

"It's important that you know why they do it."

"Why who do what?" I snapped back at him.

"Why people keep feeling they need to protect God. It makes them feel so good. How did you like the feeling of protecting the kid? Bet you got off on the martial arts comments right?"

"What are you talking about, that kid was scared shitless. You had no right to do that to him, no right at all."

"What makes you think he's a kid?" The fat man laughed.

I looked around and the boy was waving and giving me the same wink the fat man had given me.

"You mean all this was for my benefit?"

"Well you wanted to know why they do it. Why they are willing to believe they have to protect God. Now you know. It's a buzz, a wild buzz. Makes a person feel important. The bigger the thing they're protecting the bigger the buzz, and let me tell you God's pretty big. Now on top of that imagine if you started to believe that you really did knock me down. Can you imagine the ego rush that would give you?" The fat man laughed again and slapped me on the shoulder.

"Lets go grab a bite to eat. Get your bike and head down the road. There's a great little place about ten miles from here due south. Meet you there. It's called the Canary."

He turned without waiting for an answer and stepped into his car and drove away waving to the police as he drove by.

—

Chapter Eight

The Canary was a fairly nice place, at least for this part of the world. It was one of those cafes where there are actually cloth tablecloths and comfortable booths to sit at. He wasn't there when I arrived so I picked a booth looking towards the door so I would be sure to see him when he arrived.

I sat, my coffee in front of me, musing over the last few days when I heard a commotion at the front door and looking up was amazed to see the girl who had been wearing the yellow cast... and it was back on and just as bright as it had been.

She hobbled past the door thanking a couple of people who had helped her and made her way directly to my table.

"So how's it going? It looks like you get to have a coffee with me instead."

"Instead of what?" I asked, still bewildered that she would show up.

"You know exactly what I mean. So how do you like the place?"

I looked around again as I answered. "Great I suppose."

So I bet you want an explanation as to why you were involved in that little altercation back there at the rest stop right?"

"The fat guy skinny guy already told me. He said it was to show me why people want to believe that God needs protection."

"You sound a bit grumpy, are you disappointed to see me?"

"I don't even know your name, you never saw fit to tell me, even when I asked. I was expecting someone else and you showed up and all this stuff with the broken leg. That's all bull, so how do you expect me to behave?"

"Well, if you want to know the leg is actually broken. When I wear the cast the leg is broken, when I don't its not. Why else would I wear it?"

I shook my head and lifted my coffee to my lips. This was all to weird for me to even try to keep up with.

"Besides, what you choose to call me is not important, what is important is that you get some answers, right?"

She was smiling and looking so cheery that I couldn't stay grumpy any longer.

"OK, so why don't you just tell me what ever it is that I need to know and then I can be on my way?"

"Now silly, that would be a bit too easy don't you think." She smiled as she spoke.

"I suppose though that I could say that an important message in what happened to you is for you to understand how easily people can be fooled into reacting in a situation. Even you, someone who considers himself a true pacifist and has no time for anyone who is violent were moved to violence under the right circumstances."

"So what's your point?"

—

"Well the point is I wanted you to understand why people jump to these actions, like the Muslim fellow you met earlier. He was just reacting emotionally to what he thought was happening to God. That's why we all need to give ourselves permission not to believe our emotions, but that's for later."

"But like you and the other AIG's have told me. God doesn't need protecting." I ignored the bit about permissions.

She smiled again as she adjusted her leg under the table, kicking me in the process, "how do you know the boy needed protection?"

"Because I didn't know he was one of you." I stated back, a bit annoyed at the run around I kept getting from these people.

"No, you are actually wrong. The reason you moved to protect him is because you believed him to be in danger. You believed what you saw, and what you heard."

"Yes and so what. Don't most people?"

She smiled again. "That is precisely the problem and when we get to the permissions you will understand how to change it all, but that's getting ahead of ourselves."

"Oh." I said. I really didn't understand a thing she was saying but I figured that arguing or telling her anything was a waste of time.

"You're right, it would be a waste of time." She smiled, amused apparently at her ability to know my thoughts.

"Let me put it this way," she began, now serious, "People are born with the ability already there, like what you would call instinct in other animals, to have what you presently think is a connection with God. They already are spiritual creatures and they don't need religion at all. Not in the slightest. They don't need someone to tell them that they need to pray a certain way or eat something special or not eat certain things on certain days. All of that is bull, total bull invented by men who wanted to take that instinct that all people are born with and turn it to their advantage.

Like I said, everyone born already has a connection with God built in. They don't need churches or religions or religious leaders. In fact all of these things are totally contradictory to what God actually is in the first place.

"But what about Jesus or Mohammad or Buddha and all these other religious leaders?"

She shrugged, "What can I say, they are not true in the way that their religious followers believe in them. They are invented just like Betty Crocker was invented to help sell cake mix."

"Are you telling me that they never existed?"

"No they never existed, at least not in the way they are portrayed to have existed. In some cases, which I won't go into now, there were actual people and many of them actually thought they were going to do some good if they could just write down some rules for others to follow. But the truth is that people don't need rules to follow when it comes to God. They need the exact opposite."

"Have you ever wondered why so many people believe in religion and why there are so many religions?" She continued.

—

I nodded my head. "Yea, actually I have."

"The reason is that we each have an inborn connection with God. Its automatic and given to every human the moment they are born as I said a moment ago. They are all connected with God and not a one, no Pope or Iman or other religious leader is the slightest bit more connected or knowledgeable about God than you are right now. In fact I might say you are further advanced right now than most other people on this planet when it comes to understanding what is actually going on, and that's because of us of course." She smiled broadly.

"OK, if we are all connected with God why do we have such terrible things go on in the world. Why don't we all live in peace and harmony and get along?"

"The main reason is that people are all believing their thoughts and their stories. That's actually why we are talking to you now. There are many of us and we are talking to many of you and telling certain people that they need to do something about it all."

"That's all well and good but you never answered my question. Why is there not peace and harmony on earth right now?"

She smiled again and moved her hand across the table and touched me lightly. "Because most people believe what they think and what they think is that God needs protection. Its good for business."

"What do you mean? Who?"

"I won't give you names right now because you wouldn't recognize them even if I did. They are people you have never heard of and they have decided to use the connection that exists in every person to create power for themselves."

"Why, I don't understand?"

"I'm glad you said that. Most people we tell simply say, yea, power I get it. It's not what they think though. That is why we had you go through the experience with the fat man. You needed to understand that the corrupting thing about power is that you begin to believe it. You begin to believe that you actually caused something to happen. You begin to believe that you are at cause of things that happen."

"And I'm not?" I was incredulous. How could I not be at cause of at least some of the things in my life? "Are you telling me that I have no free will, that I can't decide what happens in my life?"

She smiled again. "You are so far from understanding. Let me help by giving you an example. Lets pretend that you are driving. Are you at cause of where the car goes?"

"Yes, obviously."

"But what if someone swerved in front of you and you had to suddenly change lanes?"

"OK so I had to change lanes, I don't get what you mean?"

"Were you at cause of changing lanes?"

"Yes, obviously or I would have run into the nut that cut me off."

"Did not the nut that cut you off cause you to swerve into the other lane?"

"Well, yea, I guess so if you put it that way?"

"And so you are not at cause for swerving, you are merely a link in a chain, reacting to other causes."

I sat stunned for a moment before I could answer. She was right. Every action I took or reaction I had was based on some prior action or learning or reaction. "OK so you have a point and I understand that I'm not totally at cause in that situation."

"You are not at cause in any situation at all. You are always reacting to something."

"OK, so let's just say that were true. What is the real cause of everything and why does it appear that I have free will, and if I don't have free will then who is causing all the problems in the world…God?"

"Spoken like a true agnostic, I love it." She bounced a bit in the booth as she spoke, obviously getting a real kick out of what I had said.

"Let me go back to the driving incident. Lets say you saw the guy swerve into your lane and decided for some reason not to swerve your car…what would happen?"

"I would hit him."

"Right, now would that be your choice?"

"Well according to you no, but according to me yea."

"If you had decided to hit him you would have had a reason. Some reason for not swerving to miss him, perhaps you would have been angry at him or wanted to die or who knows what."

"What if I just didn't see him?"

"Then what was it that was causing you not to see him? Where you daydreaming or thinking of a date or what? If you didn't see him that's because again, there was some thing that caused you not to see him."

"OK, I'm beginning to feel like I'm going around in circles. Is there free will or not?"

"There is not free will as long as you believe in all the crap you believe in, at least not in the way you think of it. Everyone is always reacting to something.

When people are acting in accordance with the connection with God they are allowing themselves to make decisions based on information they are getting through that connection."

I sat in silence not quite sure what to make of what she had said.

"When people hijack the name of God, like religions do all the time, then the reactions between God and people is tainted by the misinformation that is given by their own beliefs. They need to learn to simply not believe what they think."

"You mean like all the bull that is going on in the Middle East?"

"Yes, that is exactly what I mean but don't feel too superior. I don't know if you know it or not but do you remember when the Beatles records were burned because John said they were bigger than Jesus?"

I kind of remembered.

"There were crazy Christian people who thought that God needed defending then too. They thought that God needed someone to burn records because God had been injured, insulted by someone's remark. Obviously the nut cases who were burning records didn't understand that if God had wanted John not to say what he said then God would have stopped him."

I thought for a moment and then added, "So why did God allow people to burn the records?"

"For the same reason he is allowing people to fight over religion today. Because the connection has been hijacked.

"Shit, woman, don't you know people are dying everyday because of this stuff. If God is so powerful and controls everything why the hell isn't he stopping the wars and other terrible things that are happening right now?"

"First you don't understand what God is. In the way you think of him he is trying to stop it right now. You and everyone else simply are required to reinstate the connection between God and people. That's what the permissions are all about."

There she was talking about permissions, whatever they were.

"But why doesn't he just come swooping down and fix everything." I needed that answered before I would ask what she meant by the permissions.

"God does and each time the teachings have been hijacked by the religions. This has been going on for thousands of years. Miracles have decreased in size because each time they are demonstrated they are hijacked by the predominate church that is operating in the area of the miracle. Claiming that it's a miracle because of their religion. Everyone is capable of creating miracles. We all have what it takes to walk on water but we don't understand that we need to simply allow the connection to be there. To just let it happen."

"So are you telling me that we each have a destiny that we must move towards?"

She smiled again. "No, you don't have a destiny any more than it could be said that a storm cloud has a destiny. If the conditions are right then it will rain, if the conditions around it change then it won't rain. That's the wonder of the system. It is controlled but not destined."

"Hi there bud." The fat man had just arrived in the restaurant, this time in his fat persona again and I had been so intent in talking to the girl that I had missed his approach entirely.

"So, you been getting the low down on why God isn't stopping war and pestilence?"

I turned to him and smiled. "You know there is another reason, a better one really to all these problems we are all talking about and that is that God doesn't exist at all – you are all part of a very bad dream I am having and soon I will wake up and find myself cuddled up in my own bed."

"Don't think so friend" he said, and then as if to really mess me up he started to transform into his thin self right in front of me.

I shook my head. My brain hurt from this. "Why are you telling me this? Why are you doing this to me? I was just an ordinary guy and I don't understand what the deal is? Why are you picking on me? I can't do anything, or change anything or cause anything to happen. Why are you telling me all this?"

The fat man leaned across the table and looked at me for a moment and then started to talk.

"You have a lot more power than you think you do. You are going to be taking a message out to a special person and its real simple and then you can do anything you want."

I leaned back. "And what message is that?"

He smiled and sat back as he started to change into his fat self again.

"I really like being fat you know," he said mostly to himself, "You will have the message by the time you get to the hobbit hole."

I sat back. "What the hell is a hobbit hole?"

The fat man ignored me and turned to the woman.

"Oh, I have to use the can, you can fill him in I think." He said as he struggled to get out from behind the table with his huge girth.

As he waddled off to the bathroom I turned to the woman who seemed to be intent on looking out the window.

"So what is he talking about?"

"Take a look at that sky she said. One could almost think that it's going to rain again, and well, rain is not good for my cast."

I watched her intently.

She smiled and then seemed to be overcome with a serious thought as she turned back to me.

"If I was you I would turn west. There are some places that you have to see out there. I have to get going though. I'll pay the bill, you just sit here as long as you want and enjoy the view. Oh and I don't think our fat friend will be back either. You can just enjoy the view and think."

She pushed along the bench and slid out into the aisle, hobbled to the cash register, paid and then moved to the door and seemed to simply vanish.

A moment later the waitress appeared and refilled my coffee cup. "They said the meal was on them, order anything you want sugar."

I picked up the menu and took a look. I pointed at the most expensive thing that was on the menu and a beer as well. She nodded and walked towards the kitchen.

Chapter Nine

The rain had never come that day and as I leaned into the turn on the highway I felt more alive then I had in a long time. I had been on the road for almost a week now and was really getting to like it. I had stayed in a very nice B&B the first night after the talk with the fat man and the woman at the restaurant and then in a small hotel the next. I had stopped in a small town and got myself a sleeping bag, a tent and a little stove the next day deciding that I would stay outdoors for the rest of the trip if the weather continued to hold.

The mountains were fabulous and riding through them breathtaking. I rarely even thought of my old life, though it was only a few days away in the past. The constant changes of temperature and scenery as I moved up and down the passes kept me totally in the moment and every moment I seemed to be more alive then the last.

It was about an hour from sunset even though it was still early when I pulled into the small mountain town. The mountains made for an artificial twilight fairly early as the sun went below the high horizon. It was a bit cooler than I was used to because of the elevation but the place looked so nice. The bike was running well and as I throttled back I was able to look into the shop windows.

I pulled in the clutch and let the bike roll towards a parking spot in front of a small café on the corner.

Pulling the kickstand down I stood up and stretched. It had been a long ride today and though it had been magnificent somehow a chill seemed to go through me. I looked around and everything seemed perfect. It must be the twilight caused by the sun being behind the mountains that's giving me this strange feeling I thought as I took off my helmet and pushed open the café door.

The place was relatively empty and the girl at the counter motioned for me to take any seat I wanted.

I spotted a nice looking booth about half way back that afforded me a great view of the rest of the place; I always enjoyed people watching, and sat down letting the tension from the ride flow out of me.

The menu was obviously old and it looked like a thousand customers had pawed over it through the years. There were small pieces of tape over the old prices and I was temped to peel a couple off just to see what the prices had been when the menu was first printed.

"Coffee?"

The waitress was standing there coffee pot in hand. I nodded and she poured from a stainless steel carafe that had seen better days.

"Have you decided yet?"

"No not yet, is there anything you would recommend?" I asked as she stood by looking away towards the door.

"Uh, oh, no not really, everything is pretty good in here." She seemed very distracted and so I looked around her to see what seemed to be taking up so much of her attention.

—

A very short and strangely dressed man, with a short beard was leaning against the counter by the cash register up at the front of the café.

"Do you know him?" I asked the young woman.

"Kind of, she answered still staring at him". He's kind of a magician of sorts I think.

"A magician" I answered out loud. "Really."

"Yes, and a bit of trouble too. Are you ready to order now?" She moved a bit and turned her attention back to me.

"Yes, I think I will have an omelet, western."

"Good choice she said and turned on her heel." I watched her go and then looked back towards the front of the restaurant and the small man was gone.

"Excuse me, would you mind if I joined you?"

The voice was very deep but actually quite melodic as well. I swung my head around and there was the strange man behind me. How he got there was anyone's guess but he was there just the same.

"Not one bit" I answered. I was getting very used to these kinds of things now and was pretty sure that he was my next visitation.

He smelled of some kind of spice I could not name but it was very appealing and I had the urge, though I was able to keep it under control, to lean over and sniff him.

"They told me you would be arriving soon." He said.

"Oh, and who is that who told you?" I answered.

"You know, the lady with the yellow leg."

"Oh her." I answered in a matter of fact way. I had expected no less. It had been days now since I had heard from any of them and was almost thinking that I was on a real holiday.

"She's not what you really think she is you know." He said as he leaned closer

"Yes I know." I answered doing my best to get a sniff of whatever he was steeped in to try to identify it.

"She told me to give you a message."

"And what is the message?"

He leaned forward again as if to convey a great secret and whispered across the table.

"Don't believe what you hear from anyone, it's one of the permissions."

I looked at him and smiled.

"Does that mean you too?"

He looked around and smiled back as if we were sharing a great joke.

"You bet it means me too."

I thought for a second.

—

"Then if I am not supposed to listen to you why should I believe what I hear from you? Because if I believe you I won't be following your instructions and if I do listen to you I won't be following the instructions you just gave me." I smiled at my own brilliance and hoped I had said it right.

He stopped smiling and looked at me for a moment. "I thought you would be worth my time but apparently you are not. I was going to show you a trick."

I was instantly sorry for what I had said.

"I didn't mean any offense by it. It's just been a bit of a weird trip so far."

He smiled broadly again. "No pain, all is well then"

I had no idea what he meant by that but decided not to ask.

I sat there waiting for his next few words, which seemed to take a very long time in coming. The waitress walked over and refilled my cup casting a sideways glance at the fellow.

As she walked away he finally spoke again.

"Do you know why I am here?"

"No idea at all" I answered.

"I'm here to give you the first permission." He smiled and looked around and then leaned in closer. "And to show you a trick."

"Oh." I said, not really interested at all.

He waved his hands and suddenly there was a pile of money on the table.

I was very impressed, and then he waved his hands again and the money vanished.

"Not bad, what do you think?" He asked.

I was a bit put off though the trick was amazing. I was thinking back to the permissions information he had said he would share with me.

My mind shot back to the words the AIG's had said about permissions. I was very interested in what this strange man was about to say about that.

"What are these permissions and yes do tell me what the first permission is." I asked.

He looked around the room a couple of times and leaned much closer.

"The other permissions, the other nine, they aren't here. You have to get somewhere else to get them, they are in the book and you will teach them when you get to the Hobbit Hole."

He stopped talking as the waitress arrived with my meal and set it down. I waited until she had left and than leaned across the table. "What are the permissions, who are you talking about and what are they for, and yes please tell me what the first one is?"

—

For the next half hour I sat there as the strange man explained the origin of what he called the Permissions and how they were the secret of peace and the gateway to enlightenment. That once mastered those using them would have power over themselves and others in ways that were not even imaginable by most people. That it was not power born of thought or judgment, but rather power born of knowledge and wisdom. He also explained how he was not the one to tell them to me. That he knew them but that they were to be taught to me in another way.

"And what I am to do with these permissions once I find out what they are?" I asked.

"They are for your freedom from the illusion you are living in. They will free you, and you will tell him and he will share them with others."

I had no idea who he was talking about and it was obvious he was not going to tell me so I decided to ask a different question.

"And once I get free how does that help me?" I asked

"It allows you to be who you are, what you are and to experience your true self." He paused for a moment and looked around again as if expecting someone or something to suddenly burst forth. He then looked at me and repeated what he had said.

"They will free you to be who you are."

"I know exactly who I am." I answered.

He leaned over for a moment and looked around again. "That's the problem, you see you don't have any idea of who or what you are. And that means you have no idea of what you can do or what God is."

He pushed a crumpled bit of paper towards me and stood up, starting to walk away. "Find that place and you will be on your way to finding out who you are." He turned and walked away, leaving me alone in the café.

Chapter Ten

The rumble of the exhaust pipes as I rode through the tunnels was exhilarating. I figured that most of the noise was coming from the small holes in the mufflers but it was exciting non-the-less.

Only a week and half had passed since I left my car and yet it seemed like a different lifetime. The scenery was breathtaking. The deep chasms dropping hundreds of feet down the side of the mountain and the sheer mountain walls moving up the other side.

I came around a corner and slowed as I encountered a large motorhome, sluggishly making it's way along the mountain road. I followed for a while and then at the first sign of a straight patch I twisted the throttle and felt the bike respond. I leaned left and flashed past the motorhome and then back onto my side of the road.

The air was sweltering and without the movement of the bike I was sure I would have cooked. The sun beat down and the wind felt hot against my skin.

Off to my left I saw a beautiful turquoise lake and then the road swung back on itself and I was descending. The heat increased as I moved lower into the valley and the traffic got thicker too. Soon I was moving at a snails pace and seeing a fruit stand at the side of the road, I decided to take a break. I looked over my shoulder and made the turn.

I pulled into the parking lot, parked and pushed the kickstand down switching off the ignition at the same time. Swinging my leg over the handlebars I pulled my helmet off and took in a deep breath of sweet air. The scent of fruit and vegetation filled my nostrils.

There was a small building off to my right and I walked casually over there to see what it was. When I got there I discovered it was the old fruit stand, now abandoned for the one directly across the parking lot from it. Something seemed important about it though and as I lingered, looking at the weather beaten siding I saw something sticking out of one of the boards.

I reached over and pulled it out. It was an envelope, obviously stuck there some time ago, as it was yellow from the sun burning the part that was visible. I guessed it had been there a while. The overhang of the stand would have prevented the rain from getting to it and the obvious weathering of the envelope seemed to show some considerable age.

I looked around, feeling somewhat guilty for a moment because of taking the envelope and turned it over. There in block letters was my name. I felt my breath suck in as I looked at it. Clutching it in my hand I moved away from the building back towards my bike.

Sitting on my bike I looked around. Nothing seemed any different. No one had seemed to even notice my taking the letter and so I ran my finger inside of the flap and pushed it open.

Inside there was a handwritten note. It had my name at the top and then only a few lines of almost illegible writing. It read "Eat the fruit, eat as much as you can and then get on your bike and leave."

What the heck kind of note was that. I thought for a moment that I should just tear it up and get back on the bike and head off and then I thought of the strange people I had met and the events I had witnessed. I decided that no matter what I did it would turn out the same so I might as well just eat the fruit like the letter said. I headed for the fruit stand across the parking lot.

A few minutes later, sitting under a tree I started to eat the cherries I had bought. They were the only ripe fruit that was available at the time and though I was not really fond of them I had decided that if I was to eat the fruit then I would eat the fruit.

Half an hour later I was back on my bike, my stomach rumbling and I was looking intently for a motel or a gas station. If I didn't see something soon I would have to find a bush at the side of the road and with all the cars going by that was not my first choice. The cherries were beginning to give me fairly strong stomach cramps as I saw a motel in the distance.

The motel called "The Crow" was right at the end of town and as I paid for my room the clerk heard my stomach and commented that I must have been eating a lot of fruit. He turned around and pulled a small package from under the counter.

"I think you had better take this with some water, you will feel a whole lot better a whole lot fast."

"How much do I owe you for it?" I asked. He just shook his head and said that it was on the house.

Once in my room I headed for the bathroom and soon found myself deciding to take what ever the fellow had offered. In between one of my many bathroom breaks I made it to the kitchen sink and poured myself a glass of water and tore open the package. A yellow coloured substance poured out of the package forming a kind of sludge like layer on the surface of the water. I grabbed a stir stick out of the coffee cup beside the sink and gave the glass a stir and then downed it. It actually tasted kind of good. A bit medicinal but mostly orange I thought.

Almost immediately my stomachache seemed to disappear and more importantly the urgent need to run to the can seemed to be disappearing as well.

I stripped off my clothes and stepped into the shower, luxuriating in the warm water after the hot ride and long visits to the can.

Stepping out of the shower I wrapped a towel around me and was about to open my saddlebag when I felt very sleepy. I decided the best course of action was to simply slip between the sheets and get some sleep.

In a few moments I was sound asleep.

I sat bolt upright in bed, still wrapped in the towel and listened. What had woken me I wondered as I tried to get my bearings? My stomach was still gurgling a bit as I made my way to the bathroom and checked my watch. Three thirty in the morning. I had slept the whole evening away and it was the middle of the night.

As I returned from the bathroom I heard more of what had woken me, a crash and then a loud yell. Something was happening out side. I quickly threw on my clothes and then tried to see through the window. Peering outside all I could make out were streetlights, the dark shape of trees and in the distance the imposing mountains, black against the moonlight. Then it came again, another louder crash and this time a loud scream.

I opened my door and looked out. Not the brightest thing to do I thought as I stared out into the darkness and then closed the door again and moved to the phone.

Whatever is going on is work for the police I thought and picked up the phone to dial 911.

Even before I could dial a voice on the phone said hello.

"Hello, I have to make an emergency call, is this the desk?" I asked trying to get the message across that something was happening.

"No point in dialing 911," the voice continued, "the ruckus is for you."

"Who is this, are you the desk?" I almost shouted into the receiver.

"No, not the desk" the voice calmly answered. "Just a friendly reminder that you are here for a purpose and you had better get outside and straighten out the problem." The line went dead and stayed that way as I frantically tried to get a dial tone again.

Putting the phone down it was obvious that this was more of the same stuff that had been happening, so throwing on my jacket I stepped out into the cold night air.

Chapter Eleven

Almost a thousand miles away he was busy packing. The air was hot and the situation was not one that anyone would want. Busy sorting and throwing away, giving away and struggling to decide what to take and what not to take.

He was moving and was using a van and a trailer to get everything he owned out to the coast. The pace was frantic, as he only had a few days to get everything packed and ready. With no help the sweat was pouring off his face while his dog ran back and forth, excited by the prospect of a road trip.

The future ahead seemed very unsure, not a lot of money, a van with three hundred thousand miles on it and a rental trailer. All in all it didn't look too promising but things were what they were and he had to get out of there.

The boxes were lined up along the wall and it was only a couple of days until he was to depart. Today he was to take the van down to the local Uhaul and get the final touches on his hitch and then make arrangements to pick up the trailer. Not that big a trailer either as the van was old and not capable of towing a big load. Even as it was he would be dangerously overweight.

The sun was hot as he stopped to give himself a break and besides, he mused, the dog had to go for a walk. Putting her harness on he took her on a quick walk through the park, one of the last he would do there. She trotted happily along beside him and he wondered if she knew there was a very big change coming in her life.

No matter he thought. She would find out soon enough once she was stuck in the van and the two of them were on the road. No turning back, no safety net he thought as the birds chirped in the trees along the trail. His dog wandered off the path for a moment to relieve herself and as her feet touched the grass beside the path a huge swarm of mosquitoes rose into the air.

"I won't be missing them," he thought out loud as his dog squatted and peed.

Chapter Twelve

Outside the motel room the moon was very bright and as my eyes began to get accustomed to the light I could make out what seemed to be a dark shape across the parking lot. I wasn't sure what it was but as it was the only thing moving and close I decided to get a better look.

My breathing was coming in short gasps as I got closer. This was not what I was cut out for. I was not one of those AIG's and as such had no powers, no protection and really wasn't ready for whatever I would find. As I got closer, to my amazement there was nothing there but a large pile of garbage bags rippling in the wind. There was no bad smell so I figured it was not garbage but obviously it was not the source of the cries or noise either.

I stood on the street as the odd car drove by and then I looked back towards the motel from which I had come.

"Kind of scary isn't it?" The voice caught me totally off guard. I spun around to see a very harmless looking older woman standing on the sidewalk behind me.

"What, I'm sorry, what is scary?" I asked, still feeling shocked at seeing her there.

"You know what I mean. Getting out of bed hearing noises and then the voice on the phone. Makes one kind of nervous don't you think?"

It was all very obvious now. She was one of them.

"OK, so what's this one about?" I asked.

"What one," she mused as she stepped forward and took my hand. "Lets go for an early breakfast. You have to get an early start if you are going to make the coast in a few days."

"And why would I need to get to the coast in a few days?" I asked taking her hand and following her along. She was strangely warm I thought as we walked hand in hand back towards the motel. She seemed to totally ignore me so I tried a different question.

"And what was that noise?" I asked as we walked across the parking lot.

"An alarm clock. Had to get you up and ready to go one way or another." She answered with a smile.

"And why am I here anyway and why the fruit and the stomach ache and all of that?" I asked as we neared the small restaurant on the motel grounds.

"You needed to stop so you could get some sleep. We know you and if you had your way you would have kept going and it's time for a change in direction and you needed some rest. The only thing that really gets you resting is if you're not feeling that great so thus the fruit."

I nodded.

"But why not just tell me to sleep or change directions. Why the drama?"

She had let go of my hand and pulled the door to the restaurant open. There were a few truckers inside and a very weary looking waitress behind the counter.

92

"Just the two of us, a table at the back if we can." The old woman said.

"Sure lady, just pick any table you want." The waitress answered in a monotone.

We sat down and ordered and the old woman continued.

"You wanted questions answered, you wanted to know things and we wanted you to get a message out. This is just part of the message. We are here for you to learn. We'll eat and you will see exactly what I mean. Then you will be on your way." She sipped her cup of coffee and sat back waiting for our order. I had no questions and was quite frankly feeling a bit sleepy again so I just sat there looking out the window into the darkness.

After our conversation-less breakfast I sat back and realized that I felt quite good. The breakfast and early morning coffee seemed to have given me a new energy.

"Now we wait for a bit." The old woman said sitting back into her bench seat.

"Anything in particular we are waiting for?" I asked casually.

"You'll see soon enough she answered," as she lifted the coffee cup to her lips.

Not more than a minute later a man with a brown shoebox entered the restaurant and sat down at the table across from us. He seemed agitated and looked like he had not had sleep in days. His face was unshaven and his clothes looked like he had been sleeping in them for a week.

"Coffee." He said when the waitress approached him as he clutched the box tighter.

I watched him carefully, wondering what the heck was going to happen next. The box appeared to be deep brown and rather stained and abused looking. He clutched it tightly and seemed to be very worried that someone would steal it.

I was so busy watching him that I barely noticed the small man enter the restaurant and take up a seat at a forty-five degree angle from us.

The old woman tapped me on the arm to get my attention. "Now watch him, watch over there."

I turned my head around and saw the man who had just entered sitting at his table.

"Things are not ever as you think they are." She said. "That's one of the permissions. You have to give yourself permission to not believe what you think. That's permission four."

"What" I answered. "What are you talking about?"

"Just keep watching." She said nodding towards the man who had just sat down.

I started to evaluate him as I watched. He was well dressed, probably in his late thirties and it looked like he was an executive or something. He was wearing a large watch and his hair was immaculately styled as if he had just stepped out of a barbershop.

I looked down at his shoes. They were shining and looked expensive, as did his suit. Not the regular tourist or customer one would expect at four in the morning in a place like this I thought.

His face was rather drawn, as if he had some deep problem at the back of his mind but other than these things he seemed very ordinary.

"Hey mister, yea you, hey would you like to learn to invest and make some real money?" The guy with the shoebox was obviously trying to get my attention and from the way he looked I guessed he would need any money he got himself.

I was about to say something about how incongruent it all looked when she touched my arm and indicated that I needed to only watch.

I settled back into my seat. The dirty man with the shoebox had now turned his attention to one of the truckers and was asking him about investing.

"So what's the story with that guy?" I asked the woman.

"Such well chosen words." She said with a broad smile. "Story is exactly what it is. Each of us has a story and every story we have is not the truth. That man has quite a story, and you are seeing it up close and personal. The way it really is, rather then what people usually see it as."

I had no idea what she meant by that and kept watching. As I watched the guy with the shoebox got up and walked over to the trucker. To my amazement the trucker treated him with reverence and readily asked him to sit down. In a moment the two of them were busily engaged in conversation. They were close enough and talking loud enough that I could make out most of the words they were saying. It appeared from what I was hearing that the guy with the shoebox was giving the trucker advice on how to invest in the stock market and the trucker was listening!

As I watched another customer entered the restaurant and the waitress pointed to a table only a few feet from the well-dressed man sitting there minding his own business. The man who had entered looked visibly upset and leaned over towards the waitress and said in a rather loud voice. "I'm not sitting beside him, I'm sorry. Unless you have another table I'm leaving."

In amazement I watched as the waitress nodded and ushered him to a different table on the other side of the restaurant all the while apologizing for having almost sat the fellow beside the well-dressed man.

The old lady tapped me on the arm again and motioned with her head for me to look at the trucker and the guy with the shoebox.

As I turned the guy with the shoebox was happily opening the truckers' wallet right in front of him and taking all the money out and stuffing it into his dirty shoebox. The trucker seemed totally oblivious to what was happening.

"What the hell is going on here?" I whispered to the woman.

———

"Its just life as normal. The only thing is that we are using the second permission to see it all as it really is."

"What the heck do you mean by that?" I said.

"It's simple, you are seeing what is there, rather than the story. Everyone else here is just seeing the story not what is actually happening."

"I don't know what you mean?" I said. The whole thing was not making any sense to me at all.

"The second permission is for you to give yourself permission to see and hear what is really there, to not believe the stories. It lets you see what is really happening, to not believe any story, because none of them are true."

"What the hell does that mean?" I asked, getting a bit frustrated with the permission crap.

"Watch." She said and turned to me. "I need you to say something right now. Say I rescind permission two, and now only want to see the story", she paused to wait for me and then insisted again that I say it out loud."

I said the words and as I did the scene in front of my eyes changed. The well-dressed man changed into a bum, wearing old clothes and dusty shoes. He suddenly looked old and dirty, but there was still a regal air about him somehow, in his eyes I thought.

I spun my head around and the bum with the shoebox had transformed into a well-dressed businessman carrying a fancy iphone or blackberry and a briefcase. The trucker was the same and it was obvious that the trucker had always seen the shoebox man the way I was seeing him now.

"What the heck is going on here?" I asked the woman. "Are these people all AIG's?"

"No not at all. They are ordinary people. The only difference is that you were able to see them as they truly are using the second permission. By using the second permission you were able to see below the surface of what others saw. You were able to see the people the way there really were and the way the situation was really unfolding."

"I'm sorry, I still don't quite get it." I said, confused.

"You will, but you have a lot of traveling and a lot of learning to do before you get to the coast. So if I was you I would just head for your room, pack up your stuff and get on the road. Oh," she paused for a moment as she pushed a map towards me. "This is the route that you need to take by the way. Have a safe journey and happy learning's."

She got up and started to walk away. "You can get my coffee can't you?" she smiled as she turned back and was out the door in a moment.

I looked around the restaurant one more time. The shoebox man, now in a beautiful suit was still sitting with the trucker and the bum who had appeared well-dressed only minutes earlier still sat, disheveled at his table.

I put a few bills on the table, enough for the meal and a tip and headed for the door. As I passed by the table where the bum sat he reached out and touched my arm.

I stopped for a moment and looked down into his eyes. They shone with a joy I had not seen often before and he smiled at me.

—

"Have a good journey." He said and released my arm. Then he turned as I walked past and whispered in a voice that only I could hear. "You will find the answers you seek and they will be very different than you imagined." And he smiled broadly.

I smiled back, opened the door and walked slowly back to my room to put my few belonging into the saddlebags.

Chapter Thirteen

The afternoon air was wonderful. Not as hot as the day before, but warm enough to be very comfortable as I rode along. The map had taken me on what seemed to be a very roundabout path to the coast. There were switchbacks and wonderful small roads through the mountains that were fabulous.

The scenery was great and the smell of the mountain air, fresh and clean was wonderful. The traffic was less as well. Every once in a while I would see a car but most of the time the road was mine alone.

I had pulled over to the side of the road to check the map and take a short break. The sun was quite high in the sky still and so I figured I had a few hours before I had to stop for the night.

I noticed on the map that a small town ahead had a red circle drawn around it. I hadn't noticed the circle before. I quickly calculated the distance and figured it would be a good stopping off place for the evening. After putting the map away I started the bike and headed off.

A couple of hours later I was rounding a turn into the small town. It was like most places I had seen. Not much of anything in particular except for a large banner pulled across the street. On it were the words "One night only – Dr. Proud explains the mind"

The banner was blue on a white background. No instructions on where the meeting was or when for that matter.

I pulled into a service station to top up with fuel and asked the fellow filling his car next to me if he knew anything about the Dr. Proud program.

"You're in luck," he said. "The program is tonight at eight and it's only ten bucks. I'm going. It's at the community college just at the end of town. You should go." He pointed down the main street.

"Thanks I just may do that." I said and continued to fill the bike.

As the clock struck eight I found myself seated in a filled classroom holding at least fifty people. The classroom itself was not anything special. Just an ordinary classroom like you would find in any community college with a large projection screen set up for a PowerPoint presentation at the front of the room.

A couple of minutes later a rather rotund gentleman of about sixty or so walked into the room and introduced himself as a teacher at the college. He introduced Dr. Proud and as people started to clap a man much younger than I expected stood up from the front row and took the front of the room. After a moment or two there was silence.

"Thank you for the wonderful introduction," Dr Proud said, obviously at home speaking to groups of people. "I hope that you will enjoy tonight's presentation. It's all about how we perceive the world."

Over the next two hours Dr. Proud explained in great detail that we don't interact directly on the world itself. We interact through our senses and that what we see, hear and feel is not really what is there but rather our brains interpretation of it. He talked about how everything was nothing but energy vibrating and that our senses only gave us the illusion that we saw and heard and felt. That what was actually happening was that we only perceived vibrations in a giant vibrational field, and that most of the vibrations were invisible to our senses. His most amazing points were how we mixed our internal memories, ideas and beliefs with what our senses gave us. We used them to create whole new experiences that we thought were real when in fact they were no more real then dreams. They were simply a tiny bit of reality mixed with a large portion of our internal beliefs and memories.

"In closing," Dr. Proud continued. "I want you to take away from this lecture that nothing you see, hear or experience around you is really what you think is there. Everything you think you see, hear or feel is actually a mixture of outside information and inside information. And as I explained earlier, for most of us that mixture is about 20% outside information and 80% internal information making our experiences just stories we tell ourselves and really nothing at all like what reality really is."

Everyone was standing and clapping so I stood too. Thinking about it, it really was quite a thing, my mind raced as I made my way to the door. "Imagine that. Over 80% of what we think is going on in the world is not true at all. It's just our brain filling in the spaces. And the fact that the world doesn't even exist out there but rather in our own minds was totally fascinating as well."

As I was moving towards the door Dr. Proud was circulating in the room and saw me. He excused himself from the housewife he was talking to and moved directly to me.

"That's the first permission you know." He said as he approached.

I spun around. "What is the first permission?" I asked, taken by surprise. I hadn't thought that he was part of it all but apparently he was.

"That you give yourself permission to understand that we live in a bubble universe and that everything in your world exists in your head…in your own bubble if you will. You need to give yourself permission to believe that."

"Why?" I asked.

"Because it's the first stepping stone you have to understand if you are to reach the truth. When you understand that the world is really inside you your experience of the world will change and you will be privy to experiences that are beyond your imagination right now. You will learn the truth of what all the great men and woman have said, that the kingdom of heaven lies within you. When you understand the first permission you will then be ready to take the first step to enlightenment. It's the first and most powerful permission you can give to yourself. You must understand the first permission before you can understand any of the others." He gave me a wink and was on to someone else before I could ask any other questions.

I realized it was pointless trying to follow him or ask him more. If I was supposed to get more information he would show up and talk to me. If not there was no point in even trying. It seemed to work that way on this journey so I just headed out to the parking lot and got on my bike.

As I drove back to my motel I glanced up at the stars above me.

"Imagine that, all of this exists inside my own head." The immensity of it all was overwhelming.

The next morning over breakfast I examined my map more closely. There seemed to be a number of small indistinct circles that I had failed to notice earlier. Much like the circle around this very town.

It appeared that my journey was going to be punctuated by a number of stops along the way.

I paid the cashier and straddled the bike, ready for the road.

The next circled spot turned out to not be a town at all, at least not a town like I expected. It was instead an abandoned gold mine that was on the map as a tourist stop. From the look of it I would have to say that not many tourists stopped here.

There were no shops or places where someone might sit to give out information. There was no one around that I could see at all. Only a lot of dilapidated buildings and over on the far side of the property a few older structures that may have been mine buildings in their day.

I got off the bike, stowed my helmet and started to walk around the area. There was obviously some reason for me to be here and so I might as well be proactive and find it I thought.

After about half an hour of walking and looking into this and that it was plainly obvious that I was the only one there. The whole place was abandoned and though it was fun exploring the area it was not doing much for my journey.

I was on my way back to the bike when I saw something lying on the ground. It appeared to be a dark brown book of some sort. It seemed to have a leather cover and was very dirty looking like it had been there for a very long time. I bent down to pick it up.

Its cover was indeed leather and as I opened it I realized that it was handwritten and appeared to be a notebook of some sort. I thumbed through the pages looking for a name but there was none.

I walked back to the bike and rummaged in the saddlebags for a bottle of juice and some snacks. After finding them I found myself a good spot to sit, ripped open the bag of snacks and started to read.

Chapter Fourteen

The U-haul was pretty well packed, as was the van. All that was left to do was to hook the van up and take off. Tomorrow morning was the day.

He woke up the next day and hooked the van to the trailer after some difficulty in lining them up, waved his goodbyes and he and the dog pulled out of the condo parking lot and headed off to whatever lay ahead.

His money was limited and because of his budget if something went wrong along the way things could get tight. He had his credit card though, he thought as he moved along the street on the way to the highway. His dog lay down behind him in the crowded van. There was not enough room for her to really stretch out as she was on the larger side weighing in at almost 100 pounds.

It was quite an adventure for sure; one that he knew would keep him feeling a bit uncertain. A long road lay ahead, over a thousand miles and he wondered if the old van would make it. If not he was in deep trouble as there was no place to put all his belongings if he had to abandon the van or the trailer for that matter. He had very little money, a very uncertain destination and a dog to look after. Not what he would have wanted for himself if he had felt he had another choice but somehow the choices seemed to have been made for him. For good or bad he was on his way and he would handle whatever happened, be it good or bad on his own.

As the miles passed things seemed to be a lot better. He was still at least two days from the mountains so for now all that was necessary was to get as many miles as he could between him and the place he had been living. He was hurting emotionally from the situations he had left and realized that he was not really in the best of shape emotionally but that too had to be put behind him. Now was not the time for being sentimental, or for worry for that matter. What lay ahead was totally unknown. What lay behind was past and now only the open road mattered, that and his dog.

The first night was not much fun. They stopped in a small campground. It was beginning to rain and there was no reason to even try to pitch a tent. Why bother when they could sleep in the van, a plan that would prove to be less than perfect.

Cramped into the van he and the dog slept half sitting up and half stretched out on the seat. There was no room for him or the dog to really lie down. He had managed to fold one of the front seats partially down but that took up half the back seat leaving the dog virtually no place to lay in any kind of comfortable way. The two of them slept only a few hours as the rain pelted down and thunder crashed around them.

When morning came both were glad to be able to stretch and to get moving again. One more day and the mountains would be there. A new challenge for sure. He was heading for a friends place that he knew. He planned to take a break for a couple of days there, something that he looked forward to, for now though the plan was to simply drive. He needed to keep himself going and positive in the face of the move. He didn't know why but there was a deep sense of right in his leaving. He knew that he had to do it and that it would matter for some reason but as he traveled he had no idea what that reason might be.

His second night was somewhat better but still cramped. He had learned on the first night what he needed to move to be able to sleep in a more or less comfortable fashion. Things were moving along and so far everything was running to plan. Tomorrow he would be at his friends place and all would be well.

The mountains were not easy. He had traveled them many times before but never in an overloaded van of ancient vintage pulling an overloaded trailer. The engine shrieked going up the hills, at times only being able to make forty miles an hour because of the load. Every moment he felt that the engine would explode and he would be left on the side of a road, a thousand miles from everyone and everything. With no communication and the responsibility of his dog he simple mouthed a silent affirmation that they would make it and kept going.

Going down the other side of the steep hills was no better. The brakes screamed and smoked as the overloaded van and trailer slowed for traffic and tight turns around the hot mountain roads. There was no place to stop and allow the van to cool and besides, if he stopped would it start again? Together he and the dog simply kept going. The sun shining brightly as he sweated in the drivers seat. He had decided not to run the air-conditioning because of the power it drained off the engine. He needed every horse the engine could produce to keep him moving and even then there were hills that he was not sure he would make it up. Crawling slowly along at thirty miles an hour while traffic shot past him at a hundred, he could only hope that the van held out and that everything would continue to work until he got to his destination.

Finally he arrived at his friends place and a rest, not only for the van but also for him and the dog. They played and swam and enjoyed a respite before the next leg of the journey began.

On the third day after hugs and goodbyes he and the dog were again secured in the van knowing that the worst of the mountains were behind them. As to what lay ahead, that was still unknown. As it was though he was running late. He would have to pay an extra day for the trailer for sure unless he was able to make up the time he had lost going through the mountains. His time with his friends had cost him a bit of time too but it was well worth it. It was more than worth it.

Late that night his GPS told him that he was on his way to the ferry landing. It was the last leg of his journey before arriving at his final destination. If all went well for only a few more hours they would be finally arriving where they were headed. Another friend who had agreed to let him stay for a while. The future loomed uncertain but no matter what happened they were almost there.

Chapter Fifteen

The book was hard to read because the pages were written in pencil and I had a hard time making them out. But it was fairly clear that this was an instruction book of sorts. The problem was that it also seemed to be written in code of some kind. The meanings of passages were not clear and there seemed to be directions as well as instructions. There was reference to a place of sorts, beside a stream and there was an old tree and what appeared to be a cave or was it simply trees growing over a trail. I couldn't make it out exactly but I was sure that it was a description that was pointing to a very specific place. And it also talked about how it's material was to be taught. The material itself was hard to understand, as the pages seemed to not follow one another. The only thing that I could be sure of was that it was indeed an instruction manual explaining how to get someplace specific and then how to teach someone something. It seemed important and I decided that even though I didn't understand it exactly it would be important to memorize as much as possible so I could think about it as I rode.

After a bit of time trying to figure it out further I decided that it was time to move on. There was still not a sign of anyone and as far as I knew the book was the only thing that I was meant to find. It was time to get back on the road and head to the next circled destination. If I was lucky with the traffic I would make it before sunset and after trying to decipher the book I was ready for any kind of conversation that would make some sense.

I turned the bike back onto the main road and twisted the throttle feeling the power under me push me forward into the bright sunshine and empty road.

Around lunchtime I arrived at a nondescript town nestled in the foothills. The sun was shining brightly and though I was a bit tired from riding and a bit hungry I had a feeling of exuberance such as I had not had in a very long time.

The service station at the far end of town had a small restaurant and after filling the bike I swung around to the restaurant parking lot and leaned the bike over on it's stand.

Getting off the bike I reached into the saddlebags and grabbed the leather bound notebook. Might as well start the memorization process while I have a bit to eat I thought.

Inside the restaurant I settled into a bench seat, ordered and opened the book again. The sun coming through the window seemed to make it a bit easier to read and as I looked through it again I noticed something that I had failed to notice before.

Up in the right hand corner of each page was a number. I flipped through the book and found, about half way through the number one.

It was an introduction of sorts. Excited I started to read and do my best to memorize the book page by page, flipping the pages to find the next consecutive page as I read. Suddenly the book was making sense. Someone had gone to a lot of trouble to make it difficult to understand at first glance but easy to follow once you caught on. Weird I thought.

Almost three hours later I was still nursing my meal and reading with sips of coffee in between.

I had learned a lot about what had been called the Ten Permissions and was getting an idea of what the whole thing was about. The most curious part though was that interspaced with explanations of what the ten permissions were and how to use them were instructions to find someone. And even more interesting was that it was all going to take place somewhere called "the Hobbit Hole".

What the hell is a hobbit hole I thought? Sounds like something out of a Lord of the Rings story.

I ordered dessert, more because I wanted to stay and read rather than I was hungry and sat until I had finished the whole book.

I sat back in wonderment. Not only was the book something that had explained what those elusive Ten Permissions were, but it had also mentioned me and what I was going to be doing. It also said that I would change my existence and that I would not be as I thought but that I would finally find out all the answers I had wanted to have. What the hell did that mean, that I would change my existence? I wasn't sure if I liked the sound of that.

It was kind of funny actually, as I could not really remember what the heck the questions were that I had started out with. In fact the start of this journey, only days ago seemed like it was something from my childhood, or something from another life. It seemed that my old life somehow existed only as a long forgotten memory in some other dimension.

There were some things in the book that were very upsetting though. They seemed to indicate, without getting into specifics that there would be some very tough times ahead for a lot of people.

I slipped the book into my pocket and walked to the cash register to pay.

"Looked like that was some book the way you had your nose buried in it." The waitress quipped as I passed my bill over to her.

"Yea it was, I answered."

"So what's it about?" She asked as she punched the numbers into the cash register.

"Us." I answered without really thinking.

She handed me my change without another word and I turned and walked out to the bike.

The next red circle was about two hundred miles ahead. Not a long haul, only about three hours. The bike was fast and it was easy to make time as long as the road was not too twisty. The road ahead was not like a fast straight road where you could just open up, but the bike made it possible to make time. The mountain roads were less for speed and more for scenery but if you were willing to pass on the odd double line you could make up time.

With a full tank of gas I was back moving again and soon enough found the next circle. It was a camping site rather than a town and so I figured that I would just set up and do a bit of camping.

A few days before I had bought some more camping equipment and was looking forward to getting a chance to try it out anyway. I turned into the campsite and slowly cruised the site. Not many people here, which seemed odd, as it was a really pretty place. It was situated on a small stream and the sun shining through the trees presenting a dappled light shining through to the ground below.

I found what I thought was a really nice campsite and pulled in. I got off the bike and looked around. The ground was flat and clear of any rocks or roots that would poke me in the night when I was trying to sleep. One thing I didn't have was a mattress. I had a ground sheet but no mattress and so I knew that it might be a bit cold and it might also be hard. The weather was warm enough though so I figured it would be OK. I had a couple of small blankets that I put down between the tent floor and the sleeping bag to help cushion the uneven ground and give me a bit more insulation.

Once the tent was up and I was settled in I decided to take a walk around the place. It was really beautiful and I was impressed with it. On the other side of the stream there was a steep mountain slope about twenty five yards from the stream going up almost vertically. I could see that recent rain had made the hill somewhat wet and I could see places where the soil had washed away recently and others where it was still dripping. Something that surprised me as it had been so dry I thought. The cliff seemed to go up almost a thousand feet and was not a gradual slope but rather a straight up and down hillside. It didn't appear to be just rock though. It appeared to be hard packed dirt and rocks with little to no vegetation growing on the side of it.

On my side of the stream there was the campsite, and of course just past that the highway.

After walking the whole site I was really unsure why I was here. There was only one other group of campers, a family. A man, his wife and a small child and they didn't seem to take the slightest interest in me at all. Other than them there was no one else staying here and I saw nothing out of the ordinary.

I had forgotten to buy food and discovered I had only tea with me. As the evening cooled I built a fire from the wood provided by the campsite and made myself as comfortable as I could with no food. So with nothing to eat I sat their drinking tea and just watching the fire.

About eleven I was getting tired and a bit cool, at least on my back and decided to let the fire die down. I took a quick trip to a tree not far from my tent and then cuddled into the small tent and was getting ready for sleep.

It was cool in the sleeping bag. After about half an hour of tossing and turning and trying to get comfortable I got up to put my jacket and pants back on. I took the book out of my inside pocket as it was digging into me and put it up by the head of the sleeping bag and settled in feeling much more comfortable.

I had no idea what time it was. It was still pitch black but the tea that I had been drinking all night had caught up with me. My bladder was very full and I needed to get out and relieve myself.

I pulled my boots on, zipped the tent flap open and stepped outside. The stars straight up above me were beautiful and bright but the cool air hitting me reminded me I was on a mission.

I walked straight ahead almost to my bike and had just finished watering a bush when I almost fell over.

"What the hell I thought as I struggled to figure out what was happening amidst dust and debris starting to fall all around me.

I looked up and saw that the hillside on the other side of the stream was beginning to let go and I could see the dust and flow just starting to rush down the hillside from the heights above.

With my fly still open I swung my leg over my bike pushed the key into the ignition and hit the start button. As the bike sparked to life the whole hillside started to crash behind me. Without looking back I twisted the throttle and headed straight through the bush ahead of me towards the main road.

As my tires hit the pavement I leaned the bike on its side and twisted the throttle all the way. The engine screamed and the front tire started to buck upwards. I leaned forward still almost lying on my side as the powerful engine lifted the bike upright amid the rocks and dust flowing out over the road around me.

Dodging what I could I raced back along the road I had come earlier that day. I knew there was a huge rock outcropping just up ahead, not two hundred yards and I was desperate to reach it.

I looked down at the speedometer. The bike was already pushing over eighty miles an hour and the debris was catching up with me as small rocks and dust flowed out onto the road.

The road started to turn and I eased up on the throttle and leaned the bike over to make the turn. The noise was less now and the debris was no longer pushing into the road in front of me.

I rounded the corner and pulled over under the rock outcropping, my breathing coming in shallow gasps. I turned around to look but could see nothing. The darkness seemed to be everywhere. There were no more stars and it was silent except for a car alarm going off in the distance and I realized it must be the car the family had driven into the campsite.

I swung the bike around and switched on the light.

The road had totally disappeared from sight and instead of a road there was nothing but rocks and dirt piled up. There was no way I could possibly get through there now.

I sat and just looked for what seemed like a very long time though I'm sure it was only a few second and then the car alarm brought my mind back to the other campers that were still there.

"Oh my God" I mouthed and played the light around the scene by turning the handlebars. There was no place to ride to. The dusty site was at least six or eight feet high and impassable for a vehicle. I turned the bike to the side of the road and flicked the kickstand down. As I did I noticed that a part of it had been bent and then I remembered that I hadn't put it up when I started off.

Probably going through the bush saved my life. I thought that I must have hit some small bushes with the kickstand as I went through them and they had pushed it back enough so the kickstand just scraped and pushed itself back into it's place alongside the frame. Had it still been sticking out It would have caught on the road and thrown me head over heels. I would have been buried under the landslide when I leaned the bike over in my getaway I thought and shuddered.

I fumbled in my saddlebag for my flashlight and then ran for the rubble. I climbed over the first bit stumbling and falling as I went. Once around the corner I saw the whole devastation. It seemed the whole side of the mountain had fallen straight down into the stream and campground. I could see parts of the car sticking out of the rubble but not much else. The dust was still very thick and both breathing and seeing was difficult.

After only a few minutes of climbing over the rubble and yelling I began to realize that there were no answers. No sounds other than the falling rocks that seemed to keep coming down the hill every so often.

I realized this was pointless. I had no light, no equipment, no nothing. The best thing that I could do was to get help.

I scrambled back towards my bike. Upon reaching it I hit the starter and headed back towards the last town I had gone through.

I had not noticed any police station when I first drove through but I had noticed a medical center. I headed directly there thinking they would have radios.

I walked in and found one nurse on duty and quickly explained what had happened and within a few moments she had sounded the alarm.

I was checked out briefly even though I was sure I was fine and within another ten minutes the volunteer fire department was on its way to the slide. They suggested that I stay where I was as there was little I could do and they thought I might be in shock.

I was taken to a 24-hour restaurant gas station and was given coffee and some pie while the waitresses gathered around so I could tell them what had happened.

Much to my surprise I had started to shake on my way to the restaurant and by the time I had sat down I was shaking so much that I couldn't drink my coffee with out spilling it.

"Don't worry dearie," said the older of the two waitresses, "it's just your adrenalin, you will be OK in a bit. Just drink your coffee and if you spill don't give it a thought."

She was really nice I thought as my hands trembled uncontrollably.

About forty minutes later a short man in his thirties came running into the restaurant shouting that they had found the family alive. Apparently they had been saved by some large rocks that diverted the worst of the slide around them and they were alive but still trapped under the rubble. There was heavy machinery heading out there now to help in the rescue but apparently no one in the family was badly hurt at the moment.

A great cheer went up in the restaurant that had now filled with any townspeople who were not out on the road helping in the search and rescue operation or just standing around watching.

My hands had stopped shaking now and I was beginning to assess what had happened. I had no idea of how this could have happened. I reached into my pocket to pull out the map and noticed the faint red circle around the campground.

An older man with a graying hair and scruffy eyebrows moved over to my table.

"You're the fellow who gave the alarm aren't you?" He asked.

I nodded numbly and I continued to look at the map.

"Mind if I sit down?" He asked as he sat down.

I looked up and saw a big smile on his face.

I was somewhat surprised at his look and not sure what to make of it but my mind was still somewhat confused so I didn't know what to say and turned my eyes back to the map.

"I bet you're wondering why you were sent there right?"

My head snapped upright and I looked him squarely in the eye.

"Are you one of them?" I asked.

"Guilty as charged." He nodded and looked towards the waitress waving for a coffee.

"What was that about? What about those people, they could have been killed, they still are not back here. They are still in danger."

"Not to worry, it's not your business anyway. You were supposed to be there finding out some things about yourself. And how do you know they were ordinary people?"

I was staring at him as he spoke and the gravity of his words suddenly struck me. It hadn't even occurred to me that they might not be just like me, innocent bystanders in some sort of cosmic game.

"Were they?" I asked starting to get angry.

"Were they what?" He answered as the waitress brought his coffee.

"You know damn well what I mean." I said in a voice a bit too loud catching the attention of most of the people in the place.

A moment later everyone looked away. Putting my outburst down to nerves and excitement.

"Could have been. The truth is that like I said, it's not your business anyway."

"Not my business, I could have been killed and them too."

"But you weren't and neither were they." He smiled as he sipped his coffee.

"Did you read the book?" he asked.

The book. I had forgotten the book and now I realized it was buried under tons of dirt and rock back at the campsite.

"Yes, but the book…" My voice trailed off as I realized that by taking it out of my pocket I had lost it forever.

"You weren't meant to keep it, only to read it." He answered. "So did you read it? Did you get a chance to read what was written there?"

I nodded.

"Good then you know who you need to meet and what it's all about."

"No, I actually don't know any of that. I read the book and it talked about a meeting and some guy I am supposed to teach but I have no idea where this place is or how I am supposed to recognize him or anything else."

The old man turned again and waved his hand. "Could we have a bit more pie over here, for the hero, and piece for me would be great too."

The waitress nodded.

The two of us sat silently at the table for a long time. I simply didn't seem to be able to talk and he offered no comments. He simply sat there taking everything in.

About two hours later two police cars arrived and the family from the campground got out. They were ushered into the restaurant and given some food. They were dusty and dirty but otherwise appeared fine.

The waitress appeared and bent down. "They want to thank you, would you mind going over there?"

"Thank me for what?" I said.

"Without you coming for help they might have been stuck there and no one would have known." She said.

I nodded to the waitress and slid out of the seat and walked slowly over to the family sitting in the booth across the room.

As I approached the man got up and gave me a huge hug. "Thank you for doing what you did. If you had not alerted everyone to us being there we would have died I'm sure."

"It really was nothing anyone else would not have done." I said knowing it to be totally true. I returned his hug and as we parted I could see tears in his eyes. I also noticed that he was shaking. It was nice to see someone else shaking for a change.

Either he is human or one great actor I thought as I returned to my table. I was going to ask my companion a few more questions but he was gone. "Just like them to disappear as soon as a person has questions" I thought.

They told me that it would be about two days before the road was open again and that I would be put up at the local bed and breakfast until the road was open and it would be at the town's expense. I was grateful, as I had nothing left except the clothes I was wearing and the bike.

That night I slept fitfully with nightmares of giant rocks falling onto my tent and feeling the weight of boulders crushing me.

Morning didn't come fast enough.

After my shower I was feeling a lot better that is until I was going to shave and then it hit me. Everything I was traveling with was gone. My shaving kit, my first aid kit, my clothes, my pack, my tent and of course the book.

I headed downstairs and met the lady running the B&B. "Did you sleep well?" She asked.

"Actually not that well at all, but the room was terrific, just bad dreams."

"I understand." She said. "I know that there are probably lots of things you need, you know after losing most everything. The best place is the general store down past the restaurant. Come into the kitchen and have a bit of breakfast and then head down there. I bet they will be able to help you." She smiled as she gestured for me to follow her.

I was hungrier than I imagined and ate the eggs, bacon and toast she had made with gusto. I thanked her and soon I found myself back on my bike and heading down the street in search of the general store.

Once there I bought some razors, the cheap one's that come in the package of five, a few basic things and was headed back towards the bike when I saw the old man again leaning on a post across the street.

I looked around and then dashed across the street.

"So I guess you didn't sleep as well as you would have liked?" He said more as a statement than a question.

"No actually I didn't." I answered.

"Follow me, there is a nice little café around the corner and we can sit and have a bit of a chat." He turned and started to walk off. I followed him. After all what else was there to do.

Sitting down he ordered coffee and a Danish and asked if I wanted anything. I said I would have a coffee and waited for him to begin.

"So you didn't sleep well last night." He began.

"Thought we established that." I said curtly.

"Ever wonder why?" He asked as he sipped his coffee.

"Because I was almost killed last night by a bunch of big rocks and whole lot of dirt." I answered back.

"Nope, that's not it at all." He said in an annoying way.

"OK, I'll bite, what is the reason I didn't sleep well?"

He looked up at me over his coffee cup. "Were you in danger of being crushed last night?"

"What do you mean?" I said.

"It's a simple question. Was there much of a chance that you would be crushed last night? I mean after you got to the B&B?"

The town had no steep hills around it and the mountains were at least a few miles on either side of the valley. "Well actually not that much I suppose." I answered back to him.

"Then did you ever wonder why your mind is so busy worrying about something that will not happen?"

"News flash old man," I said, "I guess you missed the part where I was almost killed as were those other people last night."

He leaned over and smiled. "That was last night before the B&B. Using your logic you should have been afraid when you lay down in your tent. Were you?"

"No, " I said, "It hadn't happened yet."

"So you only worry after the fact?"

I was starting to get a bit annoyed at his line of questioning.

"What is it exactly that you are trying to tell me." I asked.

"That your mind is not at all reasonable. Last night was meant to be a powerful example of how unreasonable your mind can be. While you were in real danger your mind missed the whole thing. When you were not in any danger your mind kept you awake and gave you bad dreams. Does that sound reasonable?"

"Yes." I answered. "It was because I was given one heck of a scare."

"No." He leaned forward as he spoke. "That is not it at all. Your mind is not under your control and that is why you were not afraid when you should have been and why you were afraid when you should not have been."

"What are you talking about?" I asked, getting a bit exasperated with him.

"Do you remember the book?" He asked.

I nodded my head.

"Do you remember the last few pages, the part after the instructions on how to meet that other fellow?"

I nodded again. There was a list of words. Ten words and beside each of the ten words was the phrase "I now give myself permission to understand…"

He nodded.

"Have you noticed how much anger there is in you? How you are constantly afraid at some deep level, how you are feeling dissatisfied and unhappy. That no matter how much you get you need more to be happy?"

I didn't want to acknowledge what he was saying but I knew he was right. Here I was, alive after an avalanche of rock and dirt came crashing down on me and I was still worried about petty things. I had lived on the road going through all of these events over the past days and yet my mind was not quiet. It was constantly jumping to conclusions and wrong ideas and mostly it was filled with fear. I was always afraid on some level.

He nodded at my unspoken thoughts. "Lets take a walk." He said and started to get up. "It's time for you to learn a truth. It will take you a while to assimilate it all."

"You need to understand that you can lose everything and yet lose nothing."

"Think about that and think about how your fears all exist in your mind, no place else. You were not afraid when you were running from the slide, when you were simply experiencing, being. It was only when your mind started to think that you felt fear. That should teach you something."

He was quiet then and we walked for a long time. The sun was shining and it was warm.

Things were starting to come together in my mind. As we walked he told me how the ten words in the book were actually memory triggers for the ten permissions. He explained in a new way what the ten permissions were and how important they were to be able to leave worry, fear, pain and upset behind.

Over the afternoon I started to understand how I had been my own worst enemy. How I had judged myself and believed my story. The story about how I was hard done by and how other people had "done" things to me to make my life difficult. Losing everything changed things, even if all you lost was a sleeping bag, a tent and book. It made you think.

As we walked he went through each of the ten permissions, one by one and suddenly the book and the trip started to make sense to me. That each of the experiences that I had been through was to loosen my vice like belief in what I called reality. I learned that my idea of reality was not reality at all but rather a threadbare model of what was really out there in the world.

He spoke of how the voices in my head, what I called thinking, were constantly judging me and making me feel like I was unimportant and wrong almost all the time.

By the time we had walked and talked over the day I had a new idea of how the world worked and what had been happening. I had begun to understand that the bad events in the world, the crazy and violent and stupid one's were caused by major errors in our own thinking. And how if we were to change the world around us we needed to understand things very differently than most of us presently did.

As we headed back towards the bed and breakfast he talked about how we humans were infected with what could be called a disease of the mind. A virus in our thinking and how it was at cause for all the suffering pain and fear that we felt day in and day out. It was at cause when we were terrified when there was nothing to fear. It was at cause of our jealously and pain and doubt and every other trait that we used to punish or demean ourselves.

You need to write it all down tonight. And then you need to sleep. He had said before he said good night.

That night I wrote and wrote. I tried to get everything down that he had told me. He had said that he would meet me for breakfast and we would go out the next morning as he had one more thing to tell me. Before going to bed I put a note on the kitchen table for the landlady saying I would not be there for breakfast and went back to writing for a while.

Around three in the morning I collapsed into a deep and peaceful sleep. It was the best sleep I had ever had.

Chapter Sixteen

It was late at night as the dog and he boarded the ferry. He had decided to stay below decks with his dog so she could stretch her legs and have a few sniffs around the area. The ferry trip itself was only about one and a half hours so it really wasn't a big deal but somehow, with the darkness all around them it seemed longer.

They had returned to the van and he was sitting inside eating a banana when the whistle blew indicating they were nearing shore.

A few minutes later they were on the road once again. His cell phone was still working so he called his friend and let them know he was only half an hour or so away.

The road was crowded and he was tired, very tired. He had been driving all day and when he arrived at the townhouse his first task was to park the trailer and van in some place where it could stay for the night.

He found a place not far from where he would be staying, leashed his dog and took her across to an open field to let her relieve herself and then had his first night in their new place.

The next morning, though still very tired he had to empty the van and trailer, it was hot work but had to be done. The trailer was already a day overdue and had to be cleaned out as well and then delivered to the rental firm.

He finished, drenched with sweat around one in the afternoon, his next task was unpacking the boxes and putting things away, but not until the trailer was back at the Uhaul office.

After delivering the trailer he returned and set about the task of emptying boxes and finding places to put things. The place was already full of belongings and he found that it was more difficult than he had imagined finding places to put the things he had brought.

Between unpacking he would take his dog over to the field for her walks. He noticed trails snaking away at the back of the field across the street from their new home and promised himself that as soon as the unpacking was done he would start to explore.

By the end of the week most of the unpacking and settling in was done and he started to do some of that exploring he had promised himself. Having no idea where the trails went he simply started to walk and each day he would venture a bit further along the trails familiarizing himself with the area. The weather was warm and the walk was doing him good. He had left everything behind and the walks allowed him to clear his mind. Between walks he worked writing and putting together a program that he and his friend had decided to present to a few local people.

Somehow though it was the trails that drew him and he found himself spending hours exploring the many paths through the trees and along the stream. There was one trail though that seemed more compelling than the others, it seemed almost mystical in how the trees grew over it in a circle making it almost like a cave. He didn't go there though, he took the other trails instead as they seemed warm and open. The cave like trail seemed different, and though it looked intriguing, for now he avoided it.

Chapter Seventeen

I awoke with a start and looked at the clock. It was already ten in the morning. I had slept better than I remember sleeping in a very long time and for the first time in my life I felt a strange kind of peace over me. I thought back to the night of the avalanche and even seeing it again in my minds eye failed to arouse even the slightest bit of anguish or fear. It was as if my mind had been emptied over night and I was simply filled with a kind of bliss or happiness that was totally unfamiliar to me.

I had a leisurely shower and headed out the door. The landlady was there and waved, thanking me for the note about breakfast. I nodded and opened the door.

The sun was shining brightly and the day was alive in a way I had not experienced before. I headed down to the restaurant and sure enough, sitting on a bench outside the restaurant was the old man. As I approached him I thought that I saw a white or yellow glow around him. I rubbed my eyes figuring it was just the sun playing tricks and walked up to him.

"How are you this morning?" I asked in a cheery tone.

"Fine and I see that you are too." He smiled back as he stood up and opened the door for me to walk in first.

The breakfast was wonderful and somehow I seemed to be floating on air. I couldn't shake the feeling of excitement and joy that seemed to be part of me now. Everything seemed more colourful and brighter. The sounds around me seemed more distinct yet pleasant and things felt better. Not just my emotional feelings but things actually felt better. I found myself touching the tabletop and marveling at the texture of the wood and the linen of the tablecloth. I enjoyed the slick and shiny feel of the silverware and the white of the coffee cup. The warmth and smooth texture of the handle somehow seemed to almost make me giggle. I had no idea what was wrong with me but it felt wonderful.

At one point I almost felt I had been given some kind of drug but dismissed it as soon as I thought of it.

The old man and I talked for a long time, mostly about unimportant issues until finally he said "Remember I told you that there was one more thing that you needed to know?"

I nodded and smiled. "So what is it?"

"It's that this journey is almost over."

For a moment I was in a kind of shock. I had been feeling so good and now he was saying that it was almost over.

"What do you mean, that I am going to die?" I asked, finding that even that prospect somehow failed to dampen my spirits.

"No you are not going to die. But you are close to learning what you needed to learn and you have only one more task ahead."

I nodded to him and waited for him to continue.

"You have thought that you would be telling the world about what has happened to you and what you have found out, and you will be, but in a different way then you imagined. Your life will be changing very soon. Now don't get me wrong, you will continue to feel the way you do but your job here is almost over. There is only one more thing that you have to do and you will begin a new adventure."

"So what's the last thing I have to do?" I asked, still amazed at how good I felt.

"You must be a teacher. There is someone who is waiting for your teachings and only you can teach him. Of course you already know that but you need to know as well that your teachings will be the most important thing that will ever happen to him." He looked somber as he spoke. "After that you will embark on a very different journey into a place that is beyond your imagination."

I ignored the beyond your imagination statement and asked instead about the choice of me in all of this. "Why me, you bunch seem pretty adept at being able to get the message across." I smiled as I talked.

He smiled back and nodded. "Yes, we are, but that is not the plan. There is something else going on," he paused for a moment, "you were promised something and that promise will be kept."

I thought for a moment before answering. "Sounds good to me."

He took a small notepad out of his pocket and started to write some things on it. Then he handed it to me.

"That's a weird name." I said as I read the paper he had just passed to me.

"None the less, that's who is going to be telling people about what you have learned," he paused again for a moment as if in thought, "And he will tell people about you too. You will recognize him when you get there."

I nodded and sat back. Somehow I just felt good about it all.

"So how soon will I be able to leave?" I asked.

"The road will be open tomorrow morning, so be ready to go then. Go to the general store and get a few things, a new tent and such." He then reached into his pants pocket and pulled out his wallet and handed me two crisp hundred-dollar bills.

"My gosh, an AIG giving me money. Now that's a first." I chuckled as I took them and crumpled them into my front pocket.

After another fantastic sleep I was more than ready to hit the road. I expected to feel something, a twinge of regret or anxiousness as I rode past the slide, but nothing. I weaved between the breaks in the asphalt as I passed the area that only a couple of evenings ago had almost become my gravesite.

With the slide behind me I opened up the throttle as the road straightened out. My destination was not far away. Only a few more days and then I would meet this illusive J as I had begun to call him. I had learned to take things a day at a time and now, feeling the way I was, things seemed simple, easy and comfortable. I no longer felt alone, or anxious.

That night I stopped at another campsite. I had decided that I would try out my new tent and sleeping bag. I had also bought myself an air mattress. Snuggling down into the sleeping bag I closed my eyes and was soon fast asleep.

Chapter Eighteen

I had been traveling hard to keep to the schedule the old man had given me. I really didn't know what the hurry was but he was very specific that I needed to be there on time. Something about the time it would take to teach this fellow I was supposed to meet and how long it would take before I started this new journey of mine.

It all seemed very cloak and dagger to me, feeling the way I did now and if I had not given my word I would have simply chucked the whole thing and just headed south to enjoy myself. I had never felt this kind of freedom and joy in my life before. It eclipsed everything I had ever felt or thought I might feel. It was better than love or sex or drugs or anything else I had ever tried or thought of trying. It was a kind of peace of mind that one reads about in mystic journals. It was in a word, great.

As I rounded the corner I saw the long straight highway leading to the ferry. The speed limit stopped me from opening the throttle as much as I would have liked but it was still a wonderful feeling moving down that long finger of land set between the oceans dead calm flatness.

The lady at the terminal asked for my money and gave me a ticket. She then directed me to lane 15, especially for bikes. She had said that I would be boarding first so be prepared, as the ferry would be leaving in just a few minutes.

Soon I was sitting on the ferry astride my bike as the huge craft slowly maneuvered out of the dock. The day was so nice I had decided to stay with my bike and just watch the scenery as it floated by in front of me. I was sitting at the very front and could watch the ocean ahead through the open deck.

Sitting there I reached into my pocket and pulled out the papers the old man had given me. I was heading for a place called Victoria. Never been there, but what the heck, most of the places I had been over the last while were places I had never been and never thought I would ever be.

I read over the instructions and the names again. Funny name for a place I thought as I said the words out loud. "Hobbit Hole," weird I thought.

An hour and a half later I was on the road again heading for my destination. I knew exactly what I was supposed to do and how I was supposed to do it, and what I would find when I got there.

Thirty-five minutes later I had arrived. Pushing the bike up onto the trail I looked around. The old man had said that not only was what I was doing considered illegal, he had said that under no circumstances was I to get caught and the only danger was in those few minutes getting my bike down the trail. Keep your helmet visor down he had said. He had insisted that I buy a helmet that had a dark visor on it, and just go slow and quiet and you will be fine.

I started the bike once I was on the trail and soon was moving comfortably along the path, my visor down so as not be recognized. I had also covered my license plate with an old shirt I had bought at a thrift store just in case.

It had taken me almost an hour to get to the open field and just ahead should be the cave like entrance to the trail I was looking for. I had only about three hundred feet to go in the open before I would enter into that cave of sorts formed by the trees. Overgrown with trees and looking like the entrance to an enchanted lair it was exactly where it was supposed to be.

I looked around before I started into the open, just to make sure there were not any people or cars passing by. I went past a large green garbage container made from a 45-gallon barrel and then was into the entrance of the trail. As I passed under the overhanging trees the shadows closed in and a wonderful cool washed over me. There was a small stream on the left side and bushes and trees on the right. I drove for another minute or two and then saw what I was looking for, a flat spot down by the small river.

I turned the bike off the trail and moved towards the small meadow. There was a large tree that overhung the stream and it was a fairly steep slope down to the meadow. I got down there and turned the bike in a tight turn. It was obvious that kids used this place to play as evidenced by the tire hanging from one of the branches of the tree that stretched out over the water.

I scanned the side of the hill beside the tree and at first didn't see what I was looking for. I got off the bike to examine it closer and then I saw it, beside the trunk of the tree partly hidden by the bushes. A small opening that appeared to be nothing more than a hole in the hill.

I reached into it and found the rock the old man had told me about, grabbed, pulled and stepped back allowing the Hobbit Hole to open.

Once inside I took a good look around. It looked like someplace out of a fantasy novel. There were some stairs heading up to a loft and a small fireplace on the main floor. There was also a small window looking out that was virtually invisible from the outside.

It was a great place to spend the next while waiting for this guy whoever he was. I would study, wait and just kick back. Perhaps I would even plan what I would do next.

I pushed my bike into the place and parked it over by the wall, just as I had been instructed to do and did a bit more looking around.

A bit later I had sat down on the compact couch and just let myself relax after starting a fire. I didn't think much about where the smoke went but apparently it was well disguised, as no one seemed to notice. I would hear the odd person walking by on the trail above but most of the time it was quiet.

I had been told that I only had a few days to wait until the guy I was supposed to meet arrived. I would know him because he had a shaggy dog and would call himself by a strange name. I had it written down. Now there was nothing to do but wait.

I awoke early the next morning, or at least I thought it was early but on looking at my watch I discovered it was about eight thirty in the morning. There were people walking by above, I could hear them. It sounded like a woman and a child. Not who I was looking for.

After getting a glass of juice, the fridge came well stocked, I decided to sit down on the couch and just do a bit of reading. There were a number of spiritual books on the small shelves, most of them I had never heard of before. There was lots of reading to do and I would have some time. The fellow I was supposed to meet was not due to arrive at my door for another three days.

Chapter Nineteen

He had been avoiding that part of the trail for a while now. At least a couple of weeks and though he still felt uncertain about it, his curiosity was getting the best of him and he was wondering why it seemed so difficult to just walk down that part of the path.

It had been like he was simply not ready to enter that particular path. He would stand in the field with his dog and watch other people walk down the trail, they would disappear into the cave like entrance of trees but he somehow didn't feel right about entering it and would turn and go the other way.

That was until this day. Now he stood on the trail and something seemed to be drawing him towards the entrance. He was not sure why but he decided that if his dog wanted to go that way, today would be the day.

He put his fingers to his mouth and whistled. His dog, a huge fluffy beast with a great temperament came bounding. He bent down and whispered something to her and pointed down the trail. Her tail went up and she happily trotted in that direction, stopping short of the trees forming the entrance and looking back at him.

Chapter Twenty

Today was day three. I put on my jacket, more because I felt naked without it than because I needed it for warmth, and stepped out side. The trail looked normal enough and I took a seat on one of the big branches that overhung the stream and waited.

I had no idea if he would come or how long it would take him. I really didn't have much of an idea how I would start the conversation either. But I knew that I had to. A lot was riding on our getting together and him taking over the teaching. And I wanted my freedom back too. I had, in the short time I had been working for the AIG's gotten used to the freedom of being able to simply travel and by using the ten Permissions I had learned to live in a way that was unthinkable to me only a short time ago. No, he had to be found and convinced to do what he needed to do so I could get on with my next adventure.

I was almost dozing as I heard the footsteps on the trail and looked up. There he was, I was sure of it. The blond dog was a few feet behind him and he was walking, fairly fast along the trail gazing off into the tress.

"Nice dog" I called out as he reached a point almost opposite me on the trail above.

He stopped and looked around for a moment, not sure where the voice had come from, and then he saw me.

"Thanks he said she is a great dog. She came from the S.PC.A."

I nodded and motioned for them to come closer. I had no idea if he would think me weird or friendly, sitting there on an old tree branch.

He seemed to consider for a moment and then stepped down towards the stream. The dog pushed past him and came running up to me nuzzling my hand asking to be petted.

"You got a great spot there." He said and I nodded. "It is really. It's quite the place."

He nodded this time and I could tell he was getting ready to call the dog and start up the trail again. I had no idea if I would get another chance and because I was not free to continue my own journey until I got this started I decided to take a chance.

"Do you believe in fate?" I asked.

He stopped and looked at me for a moment, as if figuring out if the question was for real. I could also see some of his muscles start to tense.

He's readying himself in case something happens I thought…good thinking on his part.

"Well do you?" I asked again, trying to appear as non-threatening as I could, I wanted him to relax.

"I don't think so." He said, calling his dog. "Why do you ask?"

"Because I have a message for you, a very special message and it's fate that you are here to listen to me tell you."

He petted the dog on the head and seemed open to what I had to say. He apparently had scoped me out enough to feel comfortable enough to talk.

"So what is this message and who sent you to tell me?"

I laughed in spite of myself. "You would never believe it if I told you." I said, but I do need you to listen to the message. Would you do that for me?"

"I'm still standing here listening." He said.

"OK then," I began, "you have been picked to deliver a message to the world and I am the person who is going to teach you what that message is."

"And I should do this because?" He answered. He was starting to think me nuts I was sure.

"Because a lot of people and animals in the world depend on you doing it." I answered. I had been told that he had a very large soft spot for animals. That he had worked to save whales from those that hunted them and was very interested in helping dogs too.

"So, lets just say that what you are saying is correct. What the heck is this message and how do I deliver it to the world. I don't know if you are up to date on things but I am here with an old van, basically left almost everything I ever owned behind and have virtually no money. I think that perhaps you have the wrong guy." He started to turn away and move down the trail.

"No I can assure you that you are him, and don't worry about the rest of the stuff you mentioned. It will all be taken care of."

146

He stopped dead in his tracks and turned to look at me again.

"OK he said. So what exactly am I supposed to be teaching that is so important?"

I decided that it was now or never and thought frantically what I could tell him to help him to understand. I didn't have the powers that the AIG's did to manipulate things. I would have to depend on my own ingenuity and words to get him to work with me.

"OK" I started. "What would you say if I was to tell you that there is a place nearby called the Hobbit Hole and if you started to train with me there you would be able to be free of every worry and fear you experience and have what the spiritual leaders call peace of mind."

He stood there for a moment with a smile on his face. "And would there be money involved." He said, "How much is this going to cost me?"

"Not a penny out of your pocket and I would think that you would even come into enough money to do whatever was necessary, though I can't guarantee it. Heaven knows that I have been taken care of quite nicely in a number of ways but I can't guarantee that." I answered.

"OK." He answered, much to my surprise. I thought this was going to be much harder than this. He continued "I have very little to lose so I'm open to whatever you might say so lets hear it. Where do we start?"

I really was surprised and I suppose my face showed it.

"OK then," I began. "Let's start at the beginning. Lets take a walk together."

We walked and talked that first meeting for most of the day. Exploring the trails and him just listening. I told him about the girl with the yellow cast and the old man and the landslide and all the other experiences I had gone though. I told him about the biker with the suit and how I had come to be there and of course about the Hobbit Hole and about the notebook and the mission.

He nodded and simply listened. Something that I was glad about as I realized what I was saying sounded fantastic and unbelievable.

I had actually expected a lot more excuses and reasons why he couldn't do it, but strangely enough he seemed to be quite OK with the whole thing. Something that surprised me as I certainly would not have been if some weird guy living in a hole in the ground and wearing a leather biking jacket had told me that I was going to be responsible for saving people from suffering and pain all over the globe. But he seemed to take it pretty well.

By the end of the week we had begun to get down to real work, and there was a lot of real work to be done. The first thing was to have him learn everything. He had to be taught how it worked, why and what to tell people. Then he had to begin to use it. That was the real scary part for him.

But little by little he was catching on and though much of it was very different from how he had viewed the world before, he was getting it. I found that my own faith in what we were doing increased as well. As we talked and I showed him what could be done, how all the pain and anguish in our lives was actually caused by the ten factors that were covered in the permissions I began to see that the information I was teaching was more powerful than I had imagined.

———

148

We spent a lot of time over the next month walking, talking and just enjoying the trails and learning, both of us. I found that as I taught him I began to learn anew and in some ways I really began to relish our training sessions and to look forward to them.

He had begun writing and I knew why he had been picked almost right away. He was able to write and assimilate concepts faster than anyone I had ever met, including myself and I began to wonder when he would eclipse me in his knowledge. I knew it was only a matter of time. While I had required the AIG's intervention to understand some of the most basic concepts he was able to not only grasp them but use them almost immediately. His ability to go beyond what was in front of him was amazing and I knew he would succeed in this mission and why I was supposed to bow out soon. Mostly though he just needed confidence. He needed to trust his own instincts and things would be great, I was sure.

The summer went relatively fast and fall brought new levels to our training. He had mastered most of the information and he understood what I had taught him. As winter moved in he began writing and working with the material he had learned over the time we had spent together.

It was during one of our winter training periods that the first AIG showed up on the trails around the Hobbit Hole.

He told us his name was Albert. He was a slight looking man who appeared to be in his early forties. We had met him or rather J's dog had met him on the long trail out behind the Hobbit Hold. We had been walking and talking as was our custom when J's dog appeared agitated and stopped walking. She didn't growl but rather just stopped as if she had no idea what was there. Then Albert put down his hand and the dog instantly became his best friend.

J had said to him that he had not seen his dog do that before and Albert had said it was not an uncommon reaction he had on many animals. They just don't know what to make of me, he had said.

We had walked together along the trail when Albert had turned to J and simply told him that he was ready. We both stopped and looked at each other.

Albert than said, lets go back to the Hobbit Hole, there are some things that you need to know yet.

We had turned around and headed back and soon enough found ourselves sitting in the relative comfort of the Hobbit Hole around a glowing fire.

Like a typical AIG, Albert just started talking. Once we were all seated he had turned to me and told me that things were going to be changing and that I would be out of the Hobbit Hole before the end of winter but I wouldn't be doing any traveling in the way I had planned.

I said that I thought I was supposed to just do some training and then I would be free to be on my own. He smiled for a moment and told me that part of the deal had changed. It was my own decisions that had changed things.

I was a bit confused at what he said. "What do you mean I changed things?" I asked.

"Well you did. You have been thinking that just traveling a bit more is not exactly what you want. In the back of your mind you have always wanted more. You have wanted to know answers to questions that you have not even asked. You want to learn more and be more, you want to be able to see the real answers to those questions you have about reality and life itself."

"So" I said, still not understanding what all this meant.

"You don't understand what a large part your thoughts and dreams play in what happens to you. You have not quite got that part yet." Albert turned and looked at J. "He understands" motioning at J, "but you still don't. You have decided that you want more, that you want to know what the big answer is. You want the truth with a big T."

Albert passed me a small book. "This is for you" he had said and then turned his attention to J.

The dog was sitting at Albert's feet enjoying being petted. Albert smiled at J.

"It will be up to you now. You have everything you need and everything that you require to get the job done. Now there is nothing to do but for you to go out and do it."

J sat there for a moment and then said to Albert "I want to be there when it happens. You know what I mean," and he nodded towards me."

Albert stood and said, I know, you need to say good by to your friend and I understand?"

"Yes" J said with a sad look on his face.

The book Albert had given me contained the last of the instructions I would get in this dimension. After a quick glance into it while Albert was talking to J I realized what was going to happen and how my decisions and thinking had led me to this point. I was excited, terrified and happy all at the same time.

Albert continued talking to J. "Then it shall be done." Albert said. "Tomorrow we all need to be here at exactly ten in the morning. OK?" J nodded and Albert made his way to the door. At the door he stopped and turned back to me. "You don't have long, only a few hours until it's time. Be ready." I nodded and Albert stepped outside into the cold morning air.

I took another look at the book and at what my future held for me.

Chapter Twenty One

Ten o'clock arrived and we all stood outside the Hobbit Hole. Albert was wearing a dark thick coat as the snow fell heavily.

"Are you ready?" Albert asked. I nodded, as did J.

Albert stepped in between us on the trail and lifted his hands into the air. "The snow will muffle the experience to anyone around," he said.

I felt a shudder for a moment and then Albert reached over and touched my hand and J's at the same time.

For an instant I was totally knocked off balance and yet I didn't loose my footing, despite knowing what I knew I was mentally unprepared for what was happening.

I was in more than one place at the same time. I was in my life and J's life and Albert's life and someplace that I could not describe. It was bright and clean and brilliant. There were stars and yet at the same time we were on the trail.

For what seemed like a long time, though I am sure it was only an instant I could feel J stepping into my life, experiencing my experiences and learning from me and I could feel both of us stepping into Albert. We were all merged somehow and at the same time separate.

I heard Albert's voice in the distance. "We are all one, all of us." and then I was everything. I could feel everything. I could feel all the pain and joy and health and sickness in the world and beyond. I could feel the suffering of chickens and pigs in a slaughterhouse and the sexual rush of a couple making love.

My senses were overpowered and I struggled to open my eyes and then as I did I watched as J and Albert floated between the images flooding my mind and the seeming reality of the trail, then there was a great flash and I was both alone and with everything and everyone.

For a moment I was afraid and then I was calm, a calm beyond calm and in my mind a door opened. I looked back and saw Albert and J standing on the trail and at the same time I was Albert and J and knew them intimately, totally. I turned and stepped forward into the door and found myself someplace, and then I was everything.

Chapter Twenty Two

Albert shivered as snow crept down his neck as he stood on the trail. He and J were standing there alone, just the two of them.

"Where is he?" J asked.

"He is everywhere, he is where he wanted to be and now it's up to you. He won't be coming back. Soon every trace of him will be gone as if he never existed."

We walked back to the Hobbit Hole and stepped inside. The bike that had been sitting in the corner waiting for him was gone as was the saddlebag that he kept across the back of the old couch.

"You are now together, with all his knowledge, memories and more. Are you ready?"

J nodded his head and turned to look one last time at the interior of the Hobbit Hole.

"I really don't need this anymore." J said to Albert and to himself.

"I know," said Albert, once we step outside it too will be gone. All traces of him are gone except you. You carry him with you."

J nodded and together the two of them stepped out side onto the stream bank. There was a small flash of some kind, a noise, like wings flapping and the Hobbit Hole entrance was gone. All that was left was a dark mark on the tree.

"So what now?" J asked.

Albert looked upward at the slowly descending snowflakes and smiled a very large smile. "You publish the Ten Permissions and you change the world for the better, one person at a time."

Albert looked down for a moment and then continued.

"And we celebrate a very great teacher who is now where he always wanted to be." Albert bent down and touched a small tree sticking out of the snow. As he did he started to change. J watched as he went from a young woman wearing a yellow cast to a biker to an overweight waitress to a very obese man to an old man and then back to Albert, all so fast that it was hard to be sure it had happened. Albert then spoke softly, as he crouched beside the small tree. "Be well my friend and guide him for his task is immense."

Albert stood, looking exactly like Albert again and took J's arm and together they walked back along the trail as the snow fell softly on what had once been the Hobbit Hole.

On the outskirts of a town far away, the bartender looked outside and smiled as the car he had been storing for a customer slowly faded and was gone.

Epilog

So I am now finishing this book, which was started by my friend. My dog and I are getting ready for the next part of the journey, and we are hoping that you will join us on this very important path.

There has been a huge responsibility placed on all of us and each of us can, through using the Ten Permissions begin to change the world in which we live.

I have decided to place the Ten Permissions at the end of this book, as my friend would have wanted it that way. If you choose to use them they will change the way you experience the world and then with luck you may find yourself on a similar adventure to what we have taken.

I am also going to ask for your help. There is so much work to do, as the AIG's have told us, our world is not what it appears to be. We are living in an illusion, where our stories are so strong that we see them instead of each other.

We judge each other constantly and we believe what the judges in our heads tell us even though it is totally false. Because of this our lives are filled with fear and misery as we struggle day to day.

We experience emotions that we don't like and try to drown them in anything we can find.

Deep down inside most of us want more than we have because our judges tell us that we need more and we believe the judges stores. We fail to see beyond our own stories and our own struggles and we fear what we don't understand. And we don't understand anything.

We rail at God for the way the world is run and yet are unwilling to do anything to change the world for the better.

To all of you who have read this book I throw out a challenge, an opportunity for you to join me in the rest of this adventure. I offer you the chance to join me, as I was offered a chance, to learn and to become at peace with the world around us and all those that live in this world.

Please join me in attending a Ten Permissions Workshop or taking the program on line.

You have always known that you are different, that you are looking for something that you have not as yet found. You have, like so many of us been seeking and that seeking has led you to this book. Let this book lead you to the next step. Become involved in the Ten Permissions. Take the training and learn and use the Ten Permissions to set yourself and those around you free, and so begin your story anew…

Over the few pages you will find the outline of the Ten Permissions. Some people will want to use them as they are, but for many others taking a program is necessary to be able to fully understand the power behind them and how to use them. I ask that any of you that can please attend a Ten Permissions workshop to learn more about them, and how to use them. For those that can't attend a live program please take the online program that is available at the website **www.thetenpermissions.com**

If you find that you need help please email me at **justischase@gmail.com**.

Be well and the best of luck.

With love

J (Justis)

The Ten Permissions

Give yourself the permission to be who you truly are.

Permission One

Give yourself permission to understand that we live in a bubble universe and we only experience what is in our own heads. Our world is different from every other human and animal on the planet. We are unique and how we experience the world is unique to us.

Permission Two

Give yourself permission to believe nothing, not anyone else's story nor your own story. All the stories we tell ourselves are lies and nothing is really true. It's just our stories. Take nothing anyone says to you or about you personally as they are not talking about you. They are talking about a character in their story, a character that is not you. They can never really know you nor know who or what you really are.

Permission Three

Give yourself permission to transform what your judge says into something that you no longer believe. Your judge has been lying to you all your life. All the judgments about you, about how you are not good enough or not smart enough or not perfect enough are lies the judge has told you.

Permission Four

Give yourself permission to understand that what you call thinking is the judge talking – that it is NOT YOU! You can have the judge work for you or against you. There is no in-between. You must require the judge to give you only respect and love – and even then do not believe it.

Permission Five

Give yourself permission to watch your life movie in the theatre of your mind and see it as it truly is, an illusion that you have made up, simply a story. That what you think happened is not real. It is only your story of what happened. Others will have other stories and none of them are true

Permission Six

Give yourself permission to decide how you want to re-write your story. What do you want to be in your story and what kind of experiences would you like if you could write your own story. Give yourself permission to write this new story and to be willing and courageous enough to have what you really want.

Permission Seven

Give yourself permission to know that you are pure life force writing the book of your life and that you can change your own character in the story. Be this new person, and do not think it too difficult or impossible to become this person. Know that you are the main character in your book of life and because it's only a story, you can recreate your character any way you want him/her to be.

Permission Eight

Give yourself permission to understand that emotions are reactions to your judge. First you judge and then you feel an emotion from that judgment. There is nothing wrong with feeling emotions. Only strive to feel emotions from what is real, that which is being. And remember all negative emotions come directly from our belief in our judgments.

Permission Nine

Give yourself permission to be what you want to be and to do what you want to do. Do not believe your own rules. The judge made them and the rules you have about what you can and can't do are no more real than your story.

Permission Ten

Give yourself permission to understand that Self Love = Abundance. To the amount that you love yourself you create abundance Begin to love yourself so much you are willing to give yourself everything.

Biography of Justis Chase

As a speaker, trainer and writer, Justis Chase has traveled around the globe offering programs on such diverse subjects as "quantum physics and reality", "manifestation", and "spiritual awakening".

Over the past eight years Justis has offered free information, counseling and help to people around the world through his website. His landmark book on manifestation, "The Magic of Pleasure", describing how positive emotions play into the manifestation process has had many thousands of copies read worldwide.

For over twenty-five years Justis has been on the leading edge of personal transformation. He has been instrumental in creating a number of new therapeutic approaches including "Imprint Work" and is presently a director of the Milton H. Erickson Institute of Psychotherapy for British Columbia Canada. As well as teaching "The Ten Permissions", Justis also does seminars, trainings and one on one work with clients. Some of the other programs he has developed, and presented are "T.A.L.A.M", a spiritual path to manifestation, his "Magic of Pleasure" seminar series and "Tap In Break Out" a destiny change process he co-created with Dr. Brian Pound.

He has also developed a specialized dog training system based on dogs' ability to detect minute changes in people's state of mind through odor.

"The Ten Permissions" is a landmark program showing individuals, families and corporations how to create a life without suffering and how to move into a new kind of abundance where freedom exists in a way that supports personal healing, wealth, joy and spiritual awakening.

For more information on the Ten Permissions please visit "The Ten Permissions" website at **www.thetenpermissions.com**

To contact Justis personally you can email him at **justischase@gmail.com**

Made in the USA
Charleston, SC
30 August 2013